THE BOUNCING FOOTBALL
Life Lessons on the Gridiron

THE BOUNCING FOOTBALL
Life Lessons on the Gridiron

RODRIGO BARNES

ARPress
ILLUMINATING IDEAS
EMPOWERING VOICES

ARPress
45 Dan Road Suite 5
Canton MA 02021
Hotline: 1(888) 821-0229
Fax: 1(508) 545-7580

Ordering Information:

Quantity sales. Special discounts are available on quantity purchases by corporations, associations, and others. For details, contact the publisher at the address above.

Printed in the United States of America.

ISBN-13:	Softcover	979-8-89330-815-0
	eBook	979-8-89330-816-7

Library of Congress Control Number: 2024902605

TABLE OF CONTENTS

THE BOUNCING FOOTBALL:
LIFE LESSONS ON THE GRIDIRON
BY: RODRIGO BARNES

For readers who enjoy football, gravitate toward memoirs, or want insights into growing up black in the fifties, this book gives all that and more. It is a frank look into the hard knock life of a black man from his childhood in Waco, Texas, up through his National Football League career and beyond. Barnes was a 1967 college football player when school desegregation was a fresh experiment for everyone. He describes his interaction with other students: "We had a lot of adjustments to make in feeling out personal and racial boundaries..."

The author's autobiography is horrific in some parts, but Barnes doesn't seek pity. He simply says how it was, what he did about it, and how his outlook evolved. He navigated the years with style, grace, and grit. "...playing while black in Dallas at that time was terrible. In terms of living conditions and being able to grow and develop and have opportunities, Dallas just wasn't there," writes Barnes. Readers will be stunned by the strength it must've taken to have succeeded against such adversity.

For football fans, the book is extra rich. Barnes, ultimately a Super Bowl champion with the Oakland Raiders in the seventies, describes the practices, the injuries, the backroom deals, and the politics behind the scenes of the NFL. The result isn't pretty or flattering to the league. Barnes, a supreme athlete in his formative years, has reached a pinnacle again, this time as a writing talent. His book is awakening and thought-provoking. It will assuredly help any reader understand what it was like growing up as a black youth in America during the fifties and sixties. It is a poignant book describing generational trauma and healing amidst the backdrop of sports.

Part One 15
Into the World

Chapter

1

Who Am I?

As I look back on my life of seventy years, I can't help but think, *Wow. I'm still here and functioning. Praise the Lord, and thank you, God.*

I thank him also because I have a lot to look back on. I have been a champion high school and college athlete, a professional football player, and an educator, and in each, I have found a measure of success. But the successes I've had did not come easily. For every opportunity, there were challenges to overcome—some physical and economic, some mental and emotional. And each challenge offered lessons to be learned, most of them hard. By telling my life story, I hope to show that how a person handles life's challenges can mean the difference between success and failure, and that overcoming challenges adds quality to one's life, no matter what one's endeavor.

I'm going to start with my forebears because who we are as individuals has a lot to do with where we came from and the families we were born into. My father was Eddie Barnes, and my mother was Eunice Mae Hill Barnes. She was thirty when I was born, and he was a few years older. They were from Franklin, Texas, a town just north of Bryan/College Station, which was the seat of Robertson County. My father's line was from the Barnes Plantation in Woodbury, Georgia.

His paternal grandparents took the name Barnes after their "owners," as was common at the time.

Two of my mother's family lines were the Hills, from Cutoff, Georgia, and the Sheltons, from Rome, Georgia. Some of them, including my great-grandmother, supposedly were shipped there from the West Indies. This was prior to the Civil War, and they subsequently endured servitude not just to white slave owners but to Cherokee Indians as well. They worked on farms or plantations and were said to have excelled as fruit farmers and livestock ranch hands. When legalized slavery ended, the ancestors on my mother's side of the family acquired about three hundred acres of land, which they kept through Reconstruction and up until the 1920s. After that, they let go of the title to a portion of the property, some of which was eventually deeded to Berry College, a private Christian liberal arts college in Mount Berry, Georgia.

Some of the Sheltons and Hills briefly relocated to Atlanta in the 1890s, but soon after, they moved to Texas and bought around eight hundred acres of land in or near Franklin. There, my great-grandmother married a man named Lee Cathey, who was half-Indian—either Cherokee or Alabama—from East Texas, so my grandmother Ever was a mixture of black, Indian, and white. Mama, as we called her, was so light skinned and her hair was so straight that she could have passed for white, though she chose to remain in the black community.

The Hills and the Catheys made their living at farming, and I was told that, during the Great Depression, they were generous and fed a lot of people—white and black alike. They raised chickens and hogs, and their farming skills, fruit preserves, survival knowledge, and big hearts helped a lot of people during those trying times. Most of them are buried in cemeteries around Franklin and Calvert.

My mother's father was Carlton Hill. He and Mama divorced when my mother was a young girl, and Carlton moved out to Abilene, Texas, where he worked on the railroad. The water there was very hard, tasted awful, and would turn your teeth brown, so many of the residents drank only sodas. Eventually, all that soda consumption ate up Carlton's kidneys, and he died from kidney failure at age sixty-five. I was only about three, and I'd never gotten to know him. My only recollection of him alive was from a few brief visits in the days before he passed away at the Marlin, Texas, VA Hospital. My mother said he was a good man, and she seemed to have love for him although neither he nor my grandmother raised and nurtured her. Instead, her childhood was spent living with various family members, and she once told me that she'd never felt the love of a family. But I do remember standing at Carlton's burial site and seeing my mother cry and receive the American flag that had been draped over his casket. I still have that flag, although my sister, Ever, has my dad's flag. My parents married in 1938, and they subsequently found work in Waco, about an hour and a half south of Dallas. My mother was only eighteen, but my father was a little older and already had a son by a previous marriage—Bobby Eugene Barnes. Bobby, who was thirteen years older than me, remained with his mother, so I never really knew him. After he reached adulthood, Bobby served in the Navy. Maybe his service was traumatic. I'm not really sure. But afterward, he was on medication, and he subsequently had several run-ins with the police. He died while I was in college, said to have been shot in the back of the head by an LAPD cop.

At the outbreak of World War II, my father enlisted in the Army, where he shipped out to fight overseas. After the war, he returned to Waco, where I was born on February 10, 1950. I was named after Rodrigo DeTriana, a Spaniard who sailed with Christopher Columbus aboard *La Pinta*. It is believed that, on October 12, 1492, he was the first European to spot the Americas, hailing the rest of the crew with "Tiera! Tierra!" ("Land! Land!"). Two years later, I was followed by my sister, Ever Mae Barnes. I also have a younger brother, Jock, who was fathered thirteen years later, after my parents divorced. I have not seen Jock now for forty years, but I did get to hang out with him some during my football career. But that's getting ahead of myself. At that young age, I knew nothing about death or divorce, much less the pervasive reality of Jim Crow laws in America, but all three would soon influence, mold, and direct my personality and life.

California Bound

Just after Ever was born, my parents decided to move to Blythe, California, to build a new life for themselves and their growing family.

Blythe was a small town in southeastern California, right on the border with Arizona, and the weather was hot and dry. We lived in a two-bedroom duplex off a dirt road in a mostly black community down by the railroad tracks. My dad worked in restaurants as a cook and dishwasher, and my mother was a housekeeper, though she sometimes worked in the fields picking cotton and produce.

I remember playing with other neighborhood children, and though I was the youngest, the other kids were usually nice to me. But the older ones also liked to play tricks on the younger kids, and once they convinced me to eat dirt. I didn't appreciate that very much, and maybe that's what sparked my strong dislike of people taking unfair advantage of others.

I wanted to make friends with the other kids in Blythe, but our stay there was only a year and half, so I didn't have much of a chance. Though I was too young to know much about the situation, my parents were just barely making it financially, and they frequently had disputes over money. Finally, when my mother was in her early thirties, she decided to move back to Texas. Yes, my parents got a divorce. There was no fighting, loud shouting, or anger. They just decided to go their separate ways. As for me, I was a mother's boy who was about to learn firsthand how divorce can adversely affect children.

My mother, whom we called Mama Dear or Madea for short, got a job and saved up enough money for us to catch a Greyhound bus back to Waco. I was only five and didn't realize how much my life was about to change, but as we boarded the Greyhound, I felt I'd seen one phase of my life end and that another adventure would begin at the end of the bus ride. Little did I know that I was about to be thrown into an oppressive environment that was, at first, beyond my comprehension.

Back to Waco

After three days of travel, we arrived in Waco. At the time, Waco was a military town. James Connally Air Force Base sat at the city limits, and Fort Hood was an hour or so south in Killeen. The Korean War had ended just a couple of years earlier, and both it and World War II had brought an influx of all sorts of people from across the

United States to Waco and the surrounding towns. This migration opened Waco's black community to significant changes. Prior to that, Waco had been completely controlled by white culture, but the area's military personnel included people who not only had different skills and knowledge but also were of various colors and held more progressive ideas on race. On a smaller scale, it was similar to immigration today, where people coming into the United States often bring skills, techniques, and understandings that enhance and improve American culture as a whole.

The truth is, those things are going to happen regardless of the desires of some because you can't keep it out. So with the influx of all those people with their skills and fresh ideas, the Waco area couldn't help but crawl out of the little cultural swamp it had been in and that the prevailing white culture had, for years, fought to keep stagnant. Along with the increasing awareness of cultural opportunities for African Americans, there was a definite upswing in economic opportunities. In addition to the military bases themselves, General Tire and Rubber Company, A. O. Smith Bomb Company, and other businesses and military suppliers provided good jobs for African Americans—jobs that often paid union wages and offered retirement programs. Housing and other types of programs further enhanced black life in the area. Connally Air Force Base closed in 1968, but it still had a future. The facility changed hands several times in subsequent years and is now owned by the Texas State Technical College System. Home to aviation education programs, it's the largest airport in the country owned by an educational institution.

Unfortunately, the future wasn't so rosy for area African Americans. With the closing of Connally, Waco's east side was devastated. Many blacks who had been employed by the base or in one of the plants that served it lost their jobs and experienced an economic downturn. Worse for African Americans, with the loss of their economic clout, the prevailing white culture once again held sway, and what little cultural progress had been made for blacks was shed as quickly as possible. But what whites who fostered economic and cultural dominance over blacks didn't understand was that it was already too late to put African Americans back into that little bitty cultural swamp. Once ideas of social justice and economic progress enter the mind, they are difficult to eradicate.

The military base wasn't Waco's only interesting feature. Baylor University and Paul Quinn College provided higher education for the city and the surrounding area, and minor-league baseball teams from the Texas League regularly played at Katy Park, providing live games for sports fans. This was still in the era of segregation, so there were both white and black teams. I didn't get to go to the games much, and Katy Park is no longer there, but a lot of black players who later made the big time, such as Satchel Paige, Hank Aaron, and Willie Mayes, played exhibition games there.

When we first arrived in Waco, we had no place of our own to live. Although my father's mother still lived in Waco, we weren't very close to her, so that was out. Instead, we stayed with one of my mother's girlfriends for about a week. But living with the girlfriend wasn't a permanent solution. Even though my mother got a housekeeping job, she couldn't yet support Ever and me, so she took us to stay with her mother in Calvert, Texas, which was about an hour's drive southeast of Waco. The boyfriend of Madea's girlfriend took us there one evening. After we got to Calvert, we drove on for about fifteen miles before we turned onto a dirt and gravel road flanked by miles of farmland. At quarter-of-a-mile intervals, crude three-room plantation shacks sat a little way off the road, embedded in fields of cotton and corn.

At last, we approached a nice big house, and I began to think that this was going to be fun. But we didn't stop there. Instead, we turned and continued for about a mile, to pull up in front of one of those miserable plantation shacks. The yard was dirt, with sparse patches of grass and weeds. Three steps led up to a porch that spanned the front of the house. At first, I thought we might just be going for a visit, but it didn't take long for me to realize that Madea was leaving Ever and me with Mama. "I have to go make some money, and I can't pay for a babysitter," she explained before she left.

As I mentioned earlier, we called my grandmother Mama. When we first arrived in Calvert, Mama was married to a man we knew as Mr. Perry. He was an older, dark-complected man with a soft voice. He was about six feet tall and had salt-and-pepper hair that was very thin on top. At the time, he was in his midsixties, and Mama was in her early fifties. I was okay living with Mama and Mr. Perry for a week, but it wasn't long before I began to ask when Madea would come back for us. The usual response from Mama was something like, "Be quiet, boy." After enduring this sort of brusqueness for a while, I got the feeling that Mama didn't like me too much or that I was a burden to her. Mama hadn't raised my mom, so she didn't have any experience at raising kids, so maybe she just didn't know how to deal with a young boy. But she took to Ever right away, and my sister was happy since Mama began spoiling her to no end. I, on the other hand, didn't get much attention unless I got hurt, which wasn't often.

None of this sat too well with me. In a short span, I'd gone through losing my dad and moving across the country, and now I was being left in a strange place with strangers who didn't seem to like me much. I was traumatized, but I had to deal with it. Not having anyone else to turn to, I began talking to God. I wouldn't call it praying, exactly—more as if I was looking for some place to be my refuge, for someone who would listen with sympathy to my problems. And they were many. I found it difficult to adjust to the rural Texas lifestyle of the 1950s. It was a whole different world to me. This was a plantation community with no electricity or running water. There were a few wells on private property nearby, and we could sometimes get permission to pump some water, but the water tasted and smelled awful, so we had to make trips to town to get decent drinking and cooking water, which we brought home in jugs. Our house had three rooms: a bedroom, a living room with a bed, and a room for cooking, though I'm not really sure you could call it a kitchen. Since there was no water, we had to use an outhouse. One of the worst things was having to use the toilet in the middle of the night. We'd have to make our way to the outhouse by the light of a lantern or use a pot in the kitchen. Many times, I'd wake up embarrassed because I wasn't about to go out in the dark of night to the outhouse, nor was I comfortable using the pot in the kitchen.

Some people had better situations than we did since we were pretty much at the bottom and didn't have any horses, cattle, or a farm to manage. Most African Americans in the area did seasonal work. My grandmother worked in the cotton and corn fields, and the men of the community bailed hay and stacked it in the barns. Many folks raised chickens and ducks, grew fruit trees, and did some hunting and fishing to survive during the off months. A few African American families had their own farms and some livestock, and a scattering of blacks did fine as preachers, educators, and businesspeople. Doctors and lawyers were very prestigious occupations in our community, and black sports figures were popular heroes. Unfortunately, African American leadership roles were viewed and managed politically through the enforcement of Jim Crow laws.

It's important to understand the difference between segregation and what is known as Jim Crow. Segregation is the separation of different types of peoples into certain areas: whites, blacks, Italians, Asians, and so forth are often segregated in their own areas of town, for example. Jim Crow, however is another matter. Jim Crow is controlled social and economic manipulation aimed solely at African Americans and designed to discourage hope, thwart social and economic advancement, and negate any accomplishments that blacks might achieve. Under Jim Crow, justice was a word without meaning for blacks because, for us, there was no justice. So African Americans in the South were trying to develop and find some happiness and connection while living in a society with rules that constantly kept them down. If you wanted to have some rights, own property, or not be under constant threat, you had to live where those things were possible for blacks, like the East or West Coasts. The truth is that it was impossible for African Americans to catch up, much less to get ahead in the South. There was a lot of forced labor, and the costs of food, clothing, and rent constantly outstripped wages, so getting off the debit side of the Man's ledger books was never going to happen. This was true also for the Mexican field hands who did seasonal field work, but most of those folks traveled to other states because in Texas they were treated almost as badly as African Americans were. Since they weren't welcomed by the white culture, they'd usually stay in the black community and their kids attended our schools, but they wouldn't last more than a few months before they'd be gone.

The time I spent in Calvert was difficult for me. I was very lonely and had no friends or toys, so I just played with dirt and rocks and went exploring in the woods. You know it's bad when one of your major pastimes is watching the occasional traffic go by. I didn't like anything about Calvert, including the food we ate. It was all weird to me. Worse, I didn't really feel a connection with anyone. The only relief I had was Mr. Perry. I wanted a man in my life to emulate and brag about, as do all boys, and Mr. Perry spent time with me, teaching, talking, and encouraging me to learn. He had a car, and he'd take me for rides, maybe to go fishing or to go to town on Saturday. We were always going to get water, ice, or wood or taking Mama to visit her friends in Calvert, Herne, or Franklin.

Before long, my mother managed to buy a car, and she started visiting every two or three weeks. Even though we never had much, she always kept a car after that. Sometimes she'd take us to Waco for the weekend. More importantly, I was beginning to understand who and what I was in the world and what was appropriate and what was a problem. But I had a lot of questions about everything, and now the one uppermost was *why.*

CHAPTER 2

ELEMENTARY YEARS

When I was six, my mother brought me to Waco to go to school. Ever, who was only four, continued to live with my grandmother year-round until she entered first grade since Madea still couldn't afford a babysitter. I was very happy to be back with my mother and in the relative civilization of Waco. Mom had an apartment in the Cain Homes Project, which was on Waco's south side, a few blocks from the old Baylor University tennis courts.

Moving to the projects was the real beginning of the growth and development of my personality. The community was 95 percent black and was located on First and Second Streets. It was about four blocks deep, and the older buildings, which dated to the 1940s, were at the rear of the project, along a creek. They were single story and built of wood and stucco, and each had four apartments. Toward the front were the newer buildings, constructed of brick in the post-World War II era. Throughout, the apartments had from one to three bedrooms.

The projects weren't great, but they were better than where I'd been. The apartments had concrete floors raised a couple of feet above ground level, and each had a refrigerator, stove, and heater. There were two small playgrounds often filled with family activities. While all the roads in the neighborhood were gravel instead of paved, the parking lots in the project were asphalt, which gave the kids a place to skate and ride bikes. There was a black dentist, but there were no black doctors. For medical services, African Americans had to find a white doctor who would treat them. A black preacher served the religious needs of the community, and there were several black-owned or black-operated businesses, such as a corner store and a hot dog stand. Maybe the best thing for me, since I'd spent the past year in lonely isolation, was that there were other kids.

I was so happy to be with my mother that I didn't complain about anything, but really, there wasn't much to complain about, considering where I'd been living. The apartment had running water, electricity, and even better, an inside toilet—something I really appreciated after having to use Mama's outhouse. For about a month, we didn't have beds and had to sleep on pallets of newspaper, but we did have a radio, and after a few weeks, Madea acquired a couch and bunk beds. As time passed, we also got a TV and a party line telephone.

School started the week after I arrived in Waco, and I was ready to go. The school was Kurt Wilson Elementary. It was a brick building and had heating, but except for the administration offices, there was no air-conditioning. The classrooms did have floor fans, but those were always aimed at the teachers instead of the students. In the spring and summer, the temperatures inside the classrooms could exceed one hundred degrees. It was terrible, and students frequently suffered heat exhaustion or even fainted because of the heat. If they did, there was no immediate remedy because the school didn't have a nurse or any other medical personnel to examine or give care to the students.

For a couple of years now, I'd wanted to know why things were like they were and how I fit into the world, but I'd also come to realize that adults frequently lied about things to kids or withheld information. And if they were talking about adult matters and they thought you were listening, they'd say, "Get out of here. Go play somewhere. Grown folks are talking." So to find out things adults wouldn't tell me, I eavesdropped on their conversations when they thought I wasn't listening. Sometimes I'd hear conversations while I was half asleep or sitting around being quiet and pretending to be asleep. And if they made me leave, I'd often creep back to hear more of the grown-up talk. In the country houses, which were built up on cement blocks, I'd crawl underneath the rooms or porches and listen through the floor.

Depending on the adults, you did that at the risk of punishment if you were caught.

That was how I started learning about the world, but a whole a different way of doing that came when school opened up realms of knowledge, engagement, and information. Because I wanted to know the whys of everything, I was very observant, and I began to understand the meaning of some of the words that people used to describe the value and status of people. Before that understanding, I had a notion of what was good or bad—what made people happy and what not to do. One would cause people to smile and give you a reward or do you a favor, but the other would lead to punishment or some kind of unrewarding activity. By age six, I'd learned to manage basic ethics and morality, but now the formerly unknown matters of status, race, and religion began to impact my understanding of the world, further driving my quest to discover the truth about how things really were.

As I've said, I was a mama's boy, though that was definitely not what my mother needed at that time in her life. Madea got all my love, and even though she was not very affectionate, her love for me was always there. She was both my mom and dad, and I loved making her smile and laugh, and I was happy just being around her. By now, my dad was a fading memory, and my time with Mr. Perry was limited. I wanted—needed—a male mentor, but trust can be an issue, especially if you are an introverted mama's boy. All I had was Madea, and I wanted to make her proud of me, so I did well in school and always worked around the house or helped her with what she was doing.

My mother was an attractive woman and had several offers of marriage, but her suitors did not want me, though they seemed to be okay with my sister. At that time, a lot of young women were leaving their children with a grandmother while they went and started a new family with a new husband. I was always thankful that my mother kept me and endured the hardships of my development while sacrificing a more comfortable life for herself and my sister, though I kept these thoughts to myself.

I was a good student and an okay kid, but I was in need of friends. Unfortunately, I was shy from not being nurtured and given the attention I desired, and to make matters worse, I couldn't handle rejection even though I expected people not to notice or like me. I so badly wanted friends that I was sometimes disobedient and overly generous while trying to help a friend. For example, though we were dirt poor ourselves, I occasionally shared our food with hungry playmates. Since Mom was by herself and struggling to make ends meet, it hurt her when I gave away our food. I tried to deny that I had, but Madea did not tolerate lies, and a couple of whippings set me straight about not giving away items important to our survival.

By the age of six, children have been told so many tales—and lies—about life, people, and things that they are a little confused, very vulnerable, and prone to believe anything that can dazzle their young minds. Kids try all sorts of things to get the results that advertisements display. A positive or temporary fix would be all that kids needed to invest their time and energy in trying to acquire the desired results.

Understanding this fact, older kids and adults often played tricks on younger children or took advantage of their eager but narrow and inexperienced young minds. At the time, the norms of life, such as comfort, survival, communication, transportation, and entertainment, were very different for boys and girls. Girls were watched over more than boys. They were sheltered and protected, at least until their teenage years, when the girls often got married because there wasn't much else for them to do unless they had special talents. Boys, however, were more vulnerable. They were sent out into the world alone and unsupervised. They were expected to be little men by the age of twelve or thirteen.

Despite my trouble finding a male role model and the introversion I'd developed, I began to display my personality in school and around people in the neighborhood. Rodrigo was not a common name in my community, and although Madea called me Rod, I didn't know anyone named Rod who was famous. So I settled on the name Roy, after Roy Rogers. I loved Westerns, and Roy Rogers was my first and last white hero. The name stuck, and my friends— from childhood, through high school and college, and in pro sports—all called me Roy.

Diagonally behind me lived James Stafford Johnson. Our moms were friends, and early on, he was my only out-of-school friend. We met right after I came to Waco to go to school. We weren't in the same class in the first grade, but we'd play together after school. James was a few months older than me and a little bigger. He had an older brother, as I did, but at that time, he was locked up.

James and I played every day, and every other day, he'd beat me up. I didn't understand it then, but now it seems to me that his behavior often was a reaction to what had just happened to him—a sort of pecking order thing. If he had a bad day, he passed on the bad by beating me up, making him feel better. I let it go on because I needed a friend, and James was it, but that didn't mean I didn't run home crying, seeking my mother's attention and sympathy. The pain of being bullied wasn't so much physical as emotional. It hurt my feelings more than it did my body. Madea told James's mother about the problem, but that didn't change anything, and before long, I was well experienced in taking a butt whipping from James three or four days a week.

So what was my problem? Why didn't I fight back? The truth is that I was so desperate for friendship that I allowed myself to be abused by James even though I was hurt by his behavior. But there is another truth too: I just didn't have it in me to want to hurt someone. I liked my friends, and I didn't want to fight with them. It was about my inner peace and not feeling good about fighting. In a fight, someone is going to be hurt and humiliated, and I didn't want that to happen to me, nor did I want to do it to anyone else.

The environment in which I lived, though, demanded that I sometimes had to fight, and during the next three or four years, I found myself in several fights with other kids. But I wouldn't fight James even though he'd still beat me up. As time went by, that happened less frequently, and one day things came to a head. James and I were playing thump, a game in which each of us hit the other's fist until one would quit. James was very good at thumping and at not getting thumped in return, and I often was frustrated because he'd move his fist just before I'd thump. I kept telling him not to do that, but he just laughed and kept on moving his fist when I tried to thump it. Finally, I got so angry that I popped him in the eye. He put a hand over his eye and said, "I'm going to get you." I waited for him to attack, but instead, keeping his eye covered, he just walked home.

After that, James changed, and so did I. He was still James, always messing around, but now he couldn't jump on me without getting a fight in return. He was a boxer, and I was a fighter only when I was angry or forced to fight, so I never really beat him up. And over time, he actually took on others in fights on my behalf. Both of us developed other friendships, but he and I always remained best friends.

I was in the second grade when the results came in from a standard health examination we took at school. Because the examination showed some irregularities, I was sent to the hospital for a more thorough checkup. This showed that I had rheumatic fever, an inflammatory disease that can affect the heart, among other symptoms. It turned out that I had an enlarged heart and artery issues, and I was sent home for bedrest. I was not allowed to go to school, and I had to take medication three times a day. My mother tried to explain what was going on, but I didn't understand why everyone was so concerned and watchful. I felt okay, though my endurance was very low. After about six weeks, I went back to school and began limited activity. My medical condition restricted my participation in physical education and extracurricular activities, and consequently, I often felt left out and alienated from my classmates. And my home life at the time was lonely, too, because my mom was working two jobs and couldn't be the mom I needed.

For the first few years of elementary school, I was sent back to Calvert for the Christmas holidays and during summer breaks. I didn't like it much. After living in the projects, I had gotten used to electricity, indoor plumbing, and heat in the winter. Mama's house in Calvert had none of those. In the summer months, the screened porch was my bedroom, but during the Christmas holidays, I'd nearly freeze. There was a wood-burning stove in the front room, but the room where my bed was didn't have a heater, and I was the only one in that cold room. I had some heavy old quilts, but without a blanket to trap and hold body heat, they were just layers of cold fabric. During spells of freezing weather, the quilts alone wouldn't keep me warm, so I learned to sleep with old wool dress pants and shirts under my sweat suit. Every winter, a snake or two would try to find a spot near the stove or any other place in the house where it was warm. And of course, we still had to use the outhouse, rain or shine, heat or cold.

My sister, Ever, behaved pretty badly toward me, and every day, she'd get me in trouble. Mama had spoiled her, and anytime Ever hollered or acted mad, Mama would punish me. Sometimes it seemed that Ever did this just to get me in trouble for her own entertainment. It didn't matter that I hadn't done anything wrong; my explanations to Mama always fell on deaf ears, and she'd get on me. After a while, it seemed to me that Ever only wanted to torment me and that Mama didn't really like me. I believed my grandmother loved me, but I certainly was not her favorite. I didn't feel good about any of it, and I hated staying in Calvert.

Mr. Perry was still good to me, but after a couple of years, he was killed in an automobile accident after leaving a liquor store in Bremond, Texas. In those days, there were no seat belts, and he was thrown from the car, which then rolled over him. Mama had to go to identify him. Nothing had been done to make his body even a little presentable, and Mama was never the same after that. Mr. Perry had taken care of her for about thirty years, and at the time of the accident, she was in her midfifties, had no income, and was living alone on the plantation.

Soon after, Mama married a man named Gus, who was a janitor at the local black school. Gus had been friends with Mr. Perry, and his own wife had died a year earlier. I guess Mama and Gus just gravitated toward each other. Gus needed a wife, and Mama needed a man to take care of her. They seemed to have more of a partnership than a marriage. Gus, however, was not a stand-up man. Humble and with hat in hand, he always bowed down to the white will of the time. But one thing was better for me. Mama and Mr. Gus moved to town, so the location of my summer and Christmas visits changed. Though there was no commode, their house had electricity and indoor plumbing, so there were definite improvements in our living conditions.

But the area remained a pit of despair for blacks. Most were required to work in the fields or at other menial jobs for wages that were insufficient to pay for their rent and food. As a result, they were constantly in debt to the white landowners, caught in an economic trap from which there was no escape. Blacks who refused to participate were often arrested on bogus charges and then sentenced to forced labor. Consequently, many younger blacks left the area for urban centers such as Dallas, Fort Worth, and Houston to avoid forced labor and to seek education, jobs, and a better life. Occasionally, despite the difficulties imposed by the culture at the time, one of them made something more of himself. A good example is Tom Bradley, who was born in a sharecropper's log cabin just outside Calvert but who went on to serve as the first black mayor of Los Angeles, from 1973 to 1993.

Changes and No Change

When I was eight, Madea fetched Ever back to Waco to start school. Though I'd seen my sister every summer and Christmas vacation, at first, we were kind of distant. But that didn't last long. The older we grew, the more we got along, and her past behavior toward me became a distant memory. I was her protector, and I became her big brother in deed as well as name.

Ever attended Wilson Elementary too, but after only a year, we moved from the Cain Homes Project to the Estella Maxie Project on Waco's east side. This was a definite step up in our living conditions. The buildings, which covered about six square blocks, were newer and had two stories, and the apartments were larger. The environment was better, too, and more exciting in many ways. A lot of young adults and military guys with families lived there, so there were more kids, many of them older than me. And there were four playgrounds: one big and three small. A great deal was going on, and I saw and heard more, so it was a big education for me. And since my mom worked two jobs, I was left to my own devices, giving me privileges that a lot of the other kids didn't have, such as hanging out late into the night.

Those early school years marked the beginning of the growth of my personality as well as my social development. I began to learn how and where people—myself included—fit into the world. Before then, I had no idea of the effects that climates, cultures, and ecosystems had on life, liberty, and the pursuit of happiness. By now, though, I was becoming aware of some of the socioeconomic, cultural, judicial, and racial factors that influenced opportunity, personality, character, perceptions, and status. Black people, I discovered, were stereotyped by themselves as much as by whites, though those perceptions tended to vary depending on where one lived in the country or as needed by those who tried to explain the relationships—and disparities—between blacks and whites. These were all issues that a dark-skinned black boy in Texas had to come to grips with to survive, and I began to wonder if they could be overcome and if it was possible to improve my life.

All these issues, problems, and understandings were happening about the same time in my life. On a personal level, I was not happy being a poor, dark-skinned Negro. I had very few role models to guide me, and after seeing, hearing, and experiencing radical racial terrorists in police uniform, prejudiced men in judges' robes, and segregation in school systems, athletics, entertainment, and churches, I was led to wonder just whom I could trust. Why did I look like this? Why couldn't everyone be the same or appreciate one another? Why were some people so poor? Why, why, why?

The problems were pervasive. Racial tensions had always been there, though they were muffled during WWII and the Korean War. Afterward, though, they resurfaced, and with their resurgence came a loss of common respect for the law. County officials in Texas begin taking land from black farmers through land swaps, fraud, theft, and intimidation. As my ancestors and relatives died, the county either confiscated their property or forced them to sell what little remained. My mother once took my sister and me to Franklin, the seat of Robertson County, to visit her grandmother and grandfather and to view the deeds to my family's properties. She wanted to understand what was happening to our land and taxes, only to find that the situation between African Americans and the white establishment in Robertson County had become a maze of oppression. County officials claimed we had paid taxes on everyone's property but our own and that my great-grandparents had been living on the wrong property for decades. The officials said we owed back taxes and forced my great-grandparents to vacate the property.

This sort of tactic had been going on for a long time. Decades before, the county had threatened to confiscate the land, but my great-grandfather told the sheriff that if anyone tried to take his property, he'd shoot them. He was told in return that if he came to town, he would be killed. About this time, it was said that a white man my family had helped during the Great Depression sent a check to the Franklin Bank for my great-grandparents. We never verified that this was true, but the story spread throughout the county for years.

So even at an early age, I was beginning to understand that we were poor black people living in an area where Negros were without rights and laws to protect their property and families. Any expectations or dreams of success and happiness were all but destroyed by society, culture, and community norms, particularly in the South but also in other areas of the country. I found that I had a hard time understanding all the disparate conditions and privileges the different races lived under, much less accepting them. The *why* questions were growing in number in my consciousness as well as in my vocabulary.

Parents and other adults would tell you, guide you, and pull and push you to accept "your place" in whatever area, region, or society you lived—and yes, often area or region determined the social norms. Being Negro—especially in the South—was to be a social, economic, and judicial burden. Even more personally damaging, the openly dehumanizing behavior of many white people toward Negroes was worse than you can imagine because they had institutionalized social, cultural, judicial, and religious norms for teaching terror, rape, murder, and hatred. These norms were accepted as God-given for white people when dealing with Negroes, who were not considered to be human beings. A dark-skinned person living in the South—in America—was a nigger, a nigger boy, a black-ass nigger, a coon, a tar baby. And there were many more names, each one degrading, hurtful, and intended to destroy all hope and any dreams of success.

Jim Crow laws designed to keep black people "in their place" and terrorist acts were judicially supported and enforced by the white establishment and even by many blacks. Textbooks and newspapers maintained the status quo. The bottom line in the South was that it was acceptable—and even necessary and desirable—for white people to always dominate the lives of Negroes. And to cement their control, white people would bomb and burn down black churches, both vacant and occupied, and burn down black commercial buildings and schools. Any attempt by blacks to advance was met with lynching, assassinations, and burnouts. The police, judges, and white Christians in the South were allied with the radical racists, and anyone—black or white—who disagreed had better be silent or face being killed.

One time, I went out with Mr. Gus to collect firewood in the woods between Calvert and Hearne, and we walked up on a man who'd been lynched from a tree limb. After taking a close look, Mr. Gus seemed to recognize the man. We never talked about it, though. Mr. Gus wasn't about to get involved in any issues. He was well institutionalized and knew what his place was. But I remained scared for months, and I began to listen to the stories the adults told with more interest and rising concern for my personal safety.

I wasn't alone. Back then, Negroes who had to drive long distances tended to travel at night, carrying gas and food and not stopping for any reason. Stopping was dangerous. There were even published guidebooks listing safe places for blacks to stay or get gas. I'd never understood that before, but suddenly the practice made sense to me. Living in the American South was dangerous for Negroes. The women were abused, assaulted, raped, and killed, while the men were beaten, made to watch, robbed, and lynched.

Fear was always present, and for good reason since violence against blacks could erupt at any moment, anywhere, and from almost anyone, including law enforcement. My grandmother liked to have a few beers on the weekend. One Friday around six o'clock, I was with her at a beer joint owned by a Negro named Ray when the sheriff came into the club. People called the sheriff Slim because he was well over six feet and slender. Slim was around thirty-five, and he had a reputation for whipping and locking up Negro boys and men. According to gossip, Slim also had a habit of having his way with local Negro girls and married women, who gave in to his demands out of fear. It was said that Slim had done the same with Ray's wife, and that the next time Slim demanded Ray's wife sleep with him, Ray made her stay home. Whatever the reason, that day, Slim came into Ray's beer joint with an attitude. He walked right up to Ray and shot him in the head. As Ray fell down dead, Slim calmly turned and walked out of the club. Slim was never charged, though he did leave the area and move to Denton, Texas, to continue police work there. These days, and all too often, police who gun down blacks are given a few weeks of paid vacation then sent back to work. The media has made the ugliness more visible, but the norm of my youth hasn't changed much.

When I was just starting out in school, my mother looked after a few white kids—today what we might call daycare—and I was allowed to play with them. But over time, my relationship with white people changed. Even though my background and personal life experience with white people was very limited, I began to understand what it looked and felt like to experience the hatred of white people toward Negroes. To them, I was a black-ass nigger with heart disease, living in poverty in the projects with my sister and a single mother. Even before I was ten, I was almost without hope.

As you can imagine, I became confused and very disappointed at being on the bottom of the bottom in America simply because of my race. And my lack of a father figure at home bothered me too. I desperately wanted a man to help guide me and be someone I could look to for help. I tried to connect with the men living around me, but none of them seemed to want to be bothered. But sitting around with adults always helped me learn more about what was happening. Sometimes the older men felt free enough joke and talk among themselves about their military experiences, what was going on in the world, and about life in general. It wasn't what I really needed, but it was something.

What I really needed as I turned ten was to understand the truth of what was going on, especially since I was now at an age where I would have to engage with the "boss." I learned many things, and first among them was that Negros in small cities and off-the-road towns in Texas were under the unwritten Jim Crow laws. Not only were there jobs for blacks and jobs for whites, but knowing "your place" was taught to every Negro boy in the South. Fear of beatings, rapes, burnings, and lynching had destroyed most dreams and hopes of freedom, liberty, and justice in Southern blacks. If a Negro held his head up or walked and talked with style and pride, he was said to be uppity. If a white woman was walking toward a Negro, the Negro had to look down, stop walking, and maybe step off the sidewalk until she passed. Just looking in the direction of a white women could get you lynched.

Police, judges, lawyers, scholars, teachers, and preachers were members of the KKK, and I had to listen to them all describe the Negro as an inferior and inhuman species. National political, military, judicial, and religious leaders ignored the Constitution, with its promises of justice and equal treatment to all, until well after World War II. The very African American men who had fought for America during the war were being lynched on American soil by Americans. Many were killed because they wanted what was promised by government officials. My mother, teachers, and coaches often talked about the lies and promises of white Americans and the government. I was constantly reminded that the police were not my friends and protectors. Preachers often were considered to be either Uncle Toms or liars without answers to our problems. Even school textbooks reinforced the biases.

Like all Negroes in the South, I had to stay in my place around white people, and that mindset was reinforced even within the local black community. It was the Willie Lynch method of subjugation, wherein the dominant white culture used fear, intimidation, economic suppression, and lack of hope to cause the subjugated to fall into line and not only accept their subjugation but also teach others to maintain the system and subjugate themselves. There's an old racist joke that goes, "How is a bucket of [pick your minority] like a bucket of crabs? If one tries to crawl out, the rest pull him back in."

Unfortunately, there is some truth in that. Blacks were divisive with one another, and they, as much as whites, promoted and supported Jim Crow society. Negroes in my community often snitched or reported anything they knew or heard to their white masters or bosses. Many were so institutionalized that if their master died and left the gate open, they would just sit there until someone came to tell them what to do. They were as locked into their mindset as if they'd been locked in jail. Under such difficult circumstances, it was a challenge just to survive, much less grow, within our community. My own negative circumstances were compounded by the fact that if you did not have a dad visible, adults would openly refer to you as a bastard. I was very confused and felt that I'd been given a bad life to live and that there was little light or hope for me.

The years between ten and thirteen were very important. This was the time during which I began to make decisions and to guide my life with words and actions that helped direct and shape my personality. It also gave me the grit to overcome failure through hard work. But it wasn't easy, and I had to experiment with who I was and what I wanted before I came to find a better direction.

Role Models

One positive thing that happened during this time was that a few soldiers and airmen from the military bases got together and started a Boy Scout troop in the project. I was excited because this was an opportunity to have black men as mentors who could instruct us in leadership skills. These generous men took the time to help us young boys, most of whom were without dads at home, through training, discipline, encouragement, and caring. Most important, our scout leaders taught us that we were as good as or better than any people on earth. They were proud men with some experience and knowledge of the world, and I'd sit quietly, listening to every word and imagining every detail of their stories. But it wasn't all seriousness. Sometimes they would joke and lead us on, only to break out laughing at our gullibility. Naturally, we turned around and played the same trick on younger kids.

We learned a lot from our scout leaders about meeting goals and expectation. I enjoyed being around these men and hearing about their lives, families, hometowns, people they'd met, and places they'd toured during duty. And I would always ask, "Why?" I wanted to know the reasons for any decision or action taken. This sort of understanding was important to me because, at twelve, I was beginning to be a leader among my friends, but I also was at a crossroads and could see there were different ways I could go with my life. I had to decide who I was going to follow or model, what I wanted to accomplish, and how I was going to get there.

The problem was that even while I was learning positive behavior through the Boy Scouts, I also was looking down another road. My main group of friends were my age and younger. There were about eight of us, and we all lived on the same block, played together, and helped each other when we could. We seldom went to the playground, and several of the guys were members of our Scout troop. Every Saturday morning, we'd have a Scout meeting, and afterward, my friend Thomas and I would figure out how we could make some money for the week. Some of the work was legitimate, like mowing lawns, washing cars, and making trips to the neighborhood store for old people, but other things that we did for money weren't.

We targeted two phone booths that we'd jimmy open every month to collect the money inside. Also once a month, Thomas and I would catch a bus and ride to the white neighborhoods, where we'd pretend to be collecting money for one local black church or another that had been damaged by fire, weather, or hardship. The churches, of course, never saw a penny of that. We concentrated on three different areas in Waco that I'd learned about from my mother, who knew them because she cleaned houses for white people who lived there. I was always careful to avoid the houses my mother was employed to clean.

Thomas and I usually cleared fifty dollars or more each time we went to collect, and we were not used to having so much cash. I bought some clothes and kept some pocket money while Thomas spent his money on friends and kids in the neighborhood. But all that illicit money also had a downside. The kids who benefited from Thomas's generosity grew curious about where he and I were getting all that cash, and they wanted in on the hustle. Neither of us revealed the source of the money, which made our friends watch us all the more closely. Worse were the older boys. Since I had no one to protect me, older guys frequently took what money I had and used threats to force me to get more for them.

From all that, I learned a couple of important things. First, when unexpected money starts coming out, your friends aren't your friends anymore. Instead, it becomes all about the money. This showed me how lust for money can take you over and cause you to lose all sense of your character. And second, when you're a kid and you find, buy, or steal something, you have to hide it because adults make you explain how and where you got it. And your peers won't let you keep it either but will take it from you—like the older boys did to me. When you're black and living in the projects, you have to learn how to avoid problems, and having a money hustle caused problems for me—problems I didn't want or need.

During those years, all I wanted was to know, see, and do, and I didn't think anything bad could go wrong with whatever I tried. I looked for any opportunity to experience and try things I'd heard were good or different, and I emulated behaviors I saw and took things that were easy to get. I was curious and wanted to be cool, but I also was gullible, making me easily influenced.

In essence, two of my elementary school teachers laid out the parameters of my life at that time. The first was my second-grade teacher, Mrs. Sullivan. She gave me the lead role in the school's annual Easter show. I was the bunny rabbit. She took a lot of heat for doing that, I think because everyone else wanted an older kid to play the part. She stuck with me, though, and showed a lot of support, and I ended up doing a good job. I wasn't nervous at all. It gave me a chance to be somebody, and Mrs. Sullivan retains an important role in my life for encouraging me and seeing it through. Even though it was just a little school show, taking on the role was a big responsibility and something bigger than me. I derived some much-needed self-esteem from that experience, and it let me know that I had some value. It made me the star, too, which might have prodded me to think in those terms later in life. However that may be, Mrs. Sullivan had a tremendous impact and always supported me. She was the first teacher who really caught my attention.

Then later, on the East Side, I had a fifth-grade teacher who showed me another path. He also was a PE coach, and he was always raising money from his students for a football so that we could go outside and play catch. But it was really just a racket. He'd collect the money, but he'd just keep it, and we never got a football. It was funny in a way that he played us like that, and we went for it because it wasn't just us he hustled—he hustled his classes every year. It was unusual to have a teacher do that to us, but it showed that anybody might try to take advantage of you. Sometimes, all you can do is learn from bad experiences. It was tough for someone like me who didn't have an older person to give me advice about life, and I had to learn some of the harder lessons on my own.

In many ways, these two teachers, positioned like bookends near the beginning and the end of elementary school, represented the two poles of life as I saw it at the time. On one side were the people who helped and worked for you while on the other side were the people who wanted to use and take advantage of you. And as I grew and developed and began to see these polarities play out in my own life, I began to question my understanding of life and the decisions I was making—about friendships, stealing, gambling, school, lying, loyalty, accountability, and faith. I realized that all those decisions were having an impact on my character and personality.

Did I really want to continue lying, stealing, and doing all sorts of wrong things, or did I want to change my ways and try to make my dreams come true? I decided to stop tricking others and taking from them, so I quit the hustle and moved on. Besides, as Madea always said, "When everybody knows, it's time to go."

Quitting the hustle had a downside because it left me without money to buy clothes. I was growing fast and constantly needed bigger shoes and larger pants and shirts. To make ends meet, I kept mowing yards and helped others earn a few dollars. I did well enough in school, but I wasn't much for reading and writing, so I never did my best or worked hard enough to be a top student. But I have a good memory, and I tend to remember what I'm told, and friends helped me meet homework deadlines. Thanks to them and my good memory, I frequently made the honor roll and even got a couple of scholarships.

My mother's constant words to me during this time were "Good, better, best. Never let them rest. Make your good better and your better the best until your good is better and your better is the best. Give your problems and praises to the Lord. Only he can manage fear and pride." We would quote this to each other after a victory or accomplishment as well as during troubling times. Her words were powerful and seemed to make the worst of situations better, encouraging and energizing me during rigorous or stressful periods.

CHAPTER
3

FIGHT THE GOOD FIGHT OF FAITH

Though I remained confused and disappointed in my situation as a black youth in racist America, my growing faith in God helped me move forward. My mother told me about God, taught me a few prayers, and started me in Sunday school when I was five years old. She often said, "God can make a way. We give out, but we don't give up. All things are possible with God. Take your hurts and your praises before the Lord in joy." Her words encouraged me because, in God, I had someone who loved me. I understood that if I gave my life to God, he could help with all my problems. I'd also learned about Jesus Christ, the son of God, and how Jesus could make things right. Through prayer, there was hope.

One Sunday when I was about seven years old, I was sitting with Mom in church, listening to the preacher. As a usual part of his sermon, he'd invite people to come down to the front and give their lives to the Lord. I sat there, thinking about it and wondering, *Give my live to the Lord. What is this about?* And it came to me that there was something bigger than the world. As a boy, I'd often look up to see planes flying across the sky, dreaming about traveling the world, but now I realized that salvation and being with God took you to a whole different level of spiritual being. That higher level was God's world—heaven and salvation and everything we read about in the Bible. God had the answer to everything. We humans don't know what the answers are, and God doesn't explain anything beyond the words in the Bible, but we do know the answers are there and that salvation brings about support beyond the psychological and physical.

I'd also gotten to the point where I believed that God helped people who submitted to his will. I realized I didn't know how to obtain different favors or blessings, but I knew those were possible through faith in God's wisdom and love. I felt that to go to the next level of life, I had to walk down to the preacher and tell him I wanted to be baptized and give my life and be a part of God.

The baptism took place the next month. In most churches, there's a little baptismal pool behind the altar, but in our church, the pool was in the basement. We also held Sunday school down there. Those of us about to be baptized put on swimsuits and white robes, then we lined up, and the preacher asked each of us in turn, "Do you want to give your life to Christ and let Christ become the Lord of your life?" When he asked me, I said, "Yes." I said it without hesitation or doubt, and at that moment, the preacher covered my mouth and nose and took me under.

When he raised me up, I didn't feel different physically or mentally, but there's no wonder in that. Feelings and sensations are of the body, and according to the word of God, baptism does not seal the body from sickness, disease, and evil. Nor does it seal the soul, which is one's reasoning for one's actions, be they good or bad. As with the body, the soul can be damaged through bad behavior and by hurting and mistreating yourself and others—through sin. What baptism does seal, however, is the spirit, which is the real and true you, and when I came up out of the water, I felt as if my spirit was protected and saved.

But that doesn't mean that I don't have to fight against sin and its consequences, so a central question for me is, How can one save the body and soul from sin? The obvious answer is not to sin, but it's almost impossible for a person to grow up and age without committing sins. Every day is a challenge because every day is a fight of faith to protect your body and your soul from damage due to how you conduct yourself while going through good times as well as through hardships.

Nothing pleases God more than faith, but in my early years, my problem was that I thought that faith is basically emotional and psychological. We often think that we're growing older and wiser so we can handle everything ourselves, but it's not like that. As human beings, we need support to aid us in life. We don't usually recognize that, but maybe I do because I so desperately needed and wanted support the whole time I was growing up. And what I've found over time is that faith is the greatest support of all.

That's because faith is most truly a battle with how you react to situations, both positive and negative. It is the one tool that allows us to deal with all kinds of stuff. When you're battling, faith is more than just a word. Faith is how you conduct yourself to be more successful. It's getting up in the morning and fighting off the physical or emotional afflictions that are trying to tear you down and destroy you. Faith also is the knowledge and understanding that you are going to make it through whatever difficulties you find yourself in—that God will not present challenges that you can't overcome.

God's support, however, is not always seen or understood. Everybody wants to witness physical manifestations of God's work, but God manifests in the spiritual, which is invisible to us. Lacking the evidence of physical manifestations, people tend to have doubts, but even if what we need or desire is not manifested in an obvious way, that doesn't mean God is not here, aiding and supporting us.

Keeping true faith takes deep commitment and perseverance. It is very difficult to be what God says you need to be to receive what he has for you. Many of us might think we meet God's criteria, but we are far from it. You can't just go on being the same old you. You have to change yourself on a deep level to move forward. But too many of us are not fully immersed in faith, and we constantly make excuses: "I can't do that." Or "I can't do it for very long." Or "I quit." Or "I changed my mind." Or "Oh, I didn't mean today. I meant tomorrow." In making all those excuses, we're missing the fact that if you believe and have faith, then you can stand boldly, speak to your affliction or problem, and receive.

In the end, we humans don't have the answers, though we have a lot of questions. That's why every day is a test of faith in believing that you will overcome sickness, pain, and hurt and make it through the day. Some people have a farther distance to go to overcome their negative experiences because of all the careless and evil stuff they've done. I've certainly had a lot to deal with—some of it physical and behavioral, some of it psychological and emotional. How you live your life and how you achieve your successes can take tolls on your soul and your body, and what you do—for good or ill—will come back on you. So you have to understand that if you don't stop negative behaviors, don't slow down, and don't ask God to intervene, your body and soul will suffer the consequences.

Another large part of faith is patience. Patience is important because the opposite of patience is what gets you in trouble. You might not immediately see physical evidence of receiving what you desire and want to hurry things up, but trying to rush God just doesn't work. Instead, I believe that things will be all right and that those right things will come in their good time. I just have to wait for them, and how I wait affects all other aspects of faith, such as discipline. Patience leads to discipline, which is a psychological and emotional tool you can use to steady yourself and reduce anxiety and stress during trying times.

I've also learned that people act as though their understanding is the same as God's understanding, but that's not so. We might be able to touch God's spirit, but his mind and purpose are on a level far beyond us. God does not reveal himself in obvious ways but puts it on us to believe he is who he is. Unfortunately, humans are a willfully obstinate bunch, forever thinking ugly thoughts and acting on them. Not only that, most of us also want to be on top rather than to fulfill the role God has set out for us, and that, in itself, is going against God. There's only one top spot, and that belongs to him.

Sometimes, though, we succeed in finding answers to our questions, and we come to understand we have a purpose that is beyond us: to fulfill God's will and help others. And the point of that is not to bask in the praises of those we've helped but in the glory of the Lord for doing his work. That's why I'm always taking on issues on behalf of others. There's always purpose and spiritual value in trying to do the correct thing and treat people right.

Throughout life, God's help is vital. When evil comes on you, it might creep in or it might slam down quick and hard, but it will come. If people need support among themselves, they need the support of faith even more. What we, as individuals, get to do is influence others and ask God to reveal himself to them through us. That might touch only one person, but at the same time, it touches our own souls and aids our personal healing. And finally, we have to understand that God's ultimate goal is not necessarily for us to be healed, but for us to maintain long enough to accomplish the tasks he has set before us.

That's why I always say, "Fight the good fight of faith."

Chapter

4

Middle School and an Expanding World

Because Waco was a military town, its social life was popping in the early and midsixties. The excitement filtered down to younger people, and by the time I was twelve, my friends and I were partying and imitating adults. For big entertainment, there was Walker's Auditorium, which was black owned and featured concerts by musicians such as Chuck Berry, Ike and Tina Turner, B. B. King, James Brown, Aretha Franklin, and many other famous music acts. Everybody who was anybody in music went to Walker's Auditorium. For the more adventurous, a couple of other hot spots provided loads of entertainment and nightlife.

One of these, which was located between Waco and a small town named Bellmead just to the northeast, was the Sands. The Sands featured two or three gambling houses, bootlegging, food, and prostitution. Neither city claimed it, so the county sheriff had jurisdiction, but as long as he was paid off, he didn't raid the establishments. Another hot spot was Frog Town, which was on Waco's east side, near one of the city's main cattle auction barns and a meat packing plant.

The local nightclubs and beer joints were busy every weekend, filled with young adults, along with soldiers and airmen. Black people in the civilian sector were poorly paid, so a lot of women wanted to marry soldiers since they were drawing a steady paycheck, and the nightspots gave them a chance to mingle. Younger kids like me partied at home. It was a transitional time, and black communities were not seriously disrupted by the police, who didn't care if blacks went to East Waco for partying, gambling, and prostitution.

White men were more discreet. They would pick up the maids to do a little work on Saturday while their wives visited family, or on Sundays, while their wives were at church with the kids. These were their playtime hours with their black women servants. The women knew what was happening to each other, but they'd seldom speak of it. Some black men would not let their wives work because they knew the pressures that attractive women were under to provide sex. There was little else they could do because if you said too much in a small town like Waco, you could end up hurt.

My mother told me she always tried to work for white people who were older or to make friends with the wife to avoid issues, but not all black women were successful at this tactic. Several families I knew had one or two children who were off-color compared to the other members of the family. At first, I thought they might be albinos with pigmentation issues, but their other features, such as hair and eyes, showed normal coloration. I asked the kids and adults why they were so different, but no one would answer. This was puzzling to me because I wanted to be white or light skinned, and after seeing them, I thought that there might be a way to make this happen to me. I didn't know who or what I wanted to be, but I knew it was not a black-ass nigger, a tar baby, or some other defaming epithet. As the only dark-skinned member of my family, I knew only too well that nicknames could be demeaning as well as inspiring.

The years from age twelve through fourteen were very important and, in many ways, directed my character and personality in future years. This is the time when kids grow and really begin to awaken to the world, and attending middle school facilitated my development by providing answers to some of my questions about life. The school, George Washington Carver—which then housed elementary, middle, and high school, each in a different wing—is now G. W. Carver Middle School. Our teachers were good professionals, and the school's high standards were supported by our principal, J. J. Flewellen. Overall, our resources and materials were limited, but our teachers were dedicated and worked well together.

One Carver educator who helped not just me and the school, but our whole community was our then-new band director, a graduate of Prairie View A&M named Robert E. Lee Jr. (I know!) Lee began recruiting as many students as he could—and at an earlier age than before. He was on a mission to have a great high school band. I was a sixth grader at the time and wanted to be a part of something that was going somewhere, and I wasn't alone. Many younger boys and girls were excited to join. My mother went to a meeting of parents of prospective band members to find out what their kids would play and to buy the instruments. Before she went, she told me that she didn't have any extra money for an instrument, but she came home with a trombone. It was the worst horn they had, and she'd been embarrassed in front of the band director and a couple of other parents because it was all she could afford, but I was happy enough. I thanked her and began practicing on that old horn.

As is common in most schools, Carver students at each grade level took all their classes together, but it was different for the band students. We had our own classes, broken into different grade levels, and we all worked together except for special situations such as art class or advanced-learning classes for outstanding students. Mr. Lee was an exacting taskmaster with high expectations. Practice. practice, practice. He worked hard, the students worked hard, and so did the parents. And it worked. Everyone did their best to raise money to buy uniforms and better instruments and to cover travel expenses. Eventually, we had enough new uniforms for 120 marching musicians. The uniforms were black and silver with a touch of blue and were very stylish. Most of the school's prettiest girls were in the band or on the girl's drill team or were majorettes.

Over the course of two years, Mr. Lee turned a relatively inexperienced and unknown band into one of the best high school bands in the state. It looked and sounded like no other. It was a first-class band, and in those uniforms, we looked the part. He'd brought style, confidence, and touch of class to our school, and our self-assurance, skills, and appearance were beyond expectation.

As we developed, a tremendous excitement and energy surrounded the band—an energy that was quickly recognized by the community. Every time we practiced, so many parents, friends, and visitors parked by the school to watch us that cars lined the streets for several blocks all around the school. This became a regular occurrence every weekday afternoon from 3:45 to 6:30, and it was amazing to see. Even the football players, who heard us all the time, tried to finish their practice in time to sit and watch us. The drum tempos and the cadences were so cool, the brass sound was fiery and clear, and the pretty girls strutting their stuff just ignited us. The football players loved the band. It was their inspiration every time they heard the drummers kick it off, the bass step in, and the percussion tingle, setting our hips swinging and our feet strutting proudly, our heads in the air. Man, it was on for us.

While I was in middle school, I thought that it was cool to be marching in the high school band. I was traveling not just to smaller towns in the Waco area but also to big cities like Houston, Austin, San Antonio, Dallas, and Fort Worth. It was a great education for a small-town boy. One exceptional thing about our travel was that we only rode on Greyhound buses. This was riding in class at the time, and we were one of only a few school bands that traveled Greyhound to away games.

At parades, games, marching contest, concerts, or sporting events—or even if you were just hanging out at the school on weekday afternoons—you could recognize that the band produced a high-quality sound. Not only was the band very good as a whole, but also, several of its members later went on to pursue professional careers in music. We won numerous awards and contests and were recognized as one of the best high school bands in Texas for several years in a row. We even entertained crowds from around the world at Expo 67 in Montreal, Canada. Maybe most importantly, Lee brought style and a touch of class to a community that needed and wanted leadership. We always had been a competitive community, but now we were exposed to first class leadership and success. Thank you, Mr. Lee.

The band's success wasn't fully appreciated by our school coaches, though. All of a sudden, half their athletes were in the band, taking trips and having fun. The coaches didn't like the fact that some of their best players were in the band and loving it, and they might have felt that Lee's program was stealing a lot of thunder from their teams. They eventually worked out a compromise. Like some schools that let their star players play in games and march during the halftime show, we had several varsity players doing both during football season. And some of them would play sports and play in the band during concert season.

Not many of my teachers had a direct or major impact on me, but one who did was my eighth-grade teacher, Ms. Fannie B. Watson, our queen of etiquette. She'd never married and was a traditionalist with a reputation for being strict. But it was a positive sort of strictness that demanded that her students respect one another regardless of sex. The school was small, so almost all the students went through her class, and because of her, respect became an important aspect of student social life. And you'd better get it right around Ms. Watson, or she'd write it down or tell your momma. Consequently, there were few instances of boys putting down the girls or vice versa. All the kids at that school were that way thanks to Miss Watson.

Ms. Watson's insistence on our learning respect came at a critical juncture in my life. During middle school, I was consumed with the band and trying to decide what kind of person I wanted to become, but the transition from middle school to high school brought about many changes and growth in my stature and maturity. It all began suddenly, early in my ninth-grade school year, when I had an accident playing sandlot football. While I was trying to make a play, a friend of mine, Elvis Brown, turned around and blocked me below the waist. He was just trying to make a good play and wasn't trying to hurt me, but the impact broke my right leg just below my knee, an inch above the growth area.

The doctor put me in a cast and told me that my legs would not grow to the same length. I asked what he meant, and he said that the broken leg would be four or more inches shorter than the other leg. This was something I couldn't accept. I was told I had to wear the cast for ten weeks and that I was not to put any weight on the leg. I was careful to follow the doctor's directions since I wanted every chance to have my legs grow close to the same length. I lived about half a mile from school, and it was difficult carrying books while hobbling on crutches for ten weeks. But walking with crutches had an unexpected benefit because it strengthened my arms, shoulders, and back muscles.

Plus, by the Christmas holidays, I had grown from 5'4" to '10" and gained thirty pounds, surprising everyone. Thankfully, my leg grew with me.

As soon as we returned to school after the holidays, Mr. Lee called me to his office and asked what I was going to do about band. During the time I recuperated, other students had taken my horn and used it to replace parts on their own instruments, so I'd have to buy another horn or quit the band. I liked being in the band, but I knew I wasn't really a musician. My trombone skills were only average, and during my recovery, my interest in playing faded. More importantly, I realized that I was an athlete. So at the beginning of 1964, I quit the band and got into sports.

I played basketball, and that spring, I went out for the football team. This was my introduction to organized football. The coaches were a little wary at first because I'd been diagnosed with the heart condition brought on by the bout of rheumatic fever I'd had in elementary school. All I knew was that I couldn't go as long or as hard as other kids. I asked God to heal me, and I also decided to take a practical approach by doing my best to get in shape and go as long and as hard as I could. I thought that playing sports year-round would help my conditioning and endurance. My doctor and mother gave me permission to play but to rest as needed.

The coaches remained concerned, but they let me try out for the team that summer, just before my sophomore year. I was the last one to be given a practice uniform and, along with it, a new pair of shoes. Those new shoes didn't sit well with some of the older players. Since I was young and new to the team, they thought I should have a refurbished pair, but the new pair was all that was left in my size. I stowed the shoes in my locker, thinking I was equipped and ready for practice, but little did I know that would be the last time I'd see those new shoes. By the time I returned the next day, someone else on the team took them and left old ones in their place. That didn't bother me much, though. I was happy just to have a chance to play football for the school.

But school wasn't my whole life. I was young and often unsupervised since Madea was working two jobs. I needed a male role model but didn't have one, so I was willing to make friends with anyone. I hung with two other groups of guys, and each group was different. You could say they were as different as day and night since I hung out with my neighborhood friends during the day and a rougher crew after hours.

This second group I hung out with were guys who lived in Sand Town, which was the neighborhood next to the Sands. These guys were not good students, and they seldom went to school. They wanted to run the streets, and they might work hard for a day or so at menial jobs, but mostly they'd steal or pick up the crumbs and leftovers that grown-ups overlooked. Everybody in that crew was always watching like vultures to see if anyone else would slip up or fail to keep pace with the action. Although we were running together, if trouble came, you probably were on your own. Most of the time, I stayed out of the way, and truthfully, I was there mostly to chase the girls. It was a lot of fun, but eventually I came to dislike the situation I was getting into, so I decided to return to my local group. They were younger and slower, but they weren't setting me up or ripping me off.

Eddie was in my neighborhood group. He was tall and had a sharp mind and a quick tongue. Eddie's brother, Larry, was my younger buddy. We all hung out during the summer, and for a while, it was almost as if they had a third brother. Eddie and Larry had an uncle nicknamed Footlong. Footlong was a local hustler with a crew of five: three guys and two ladies. Footlong was about 5'10", and his buddy Chris was about the same, but the third guy, John, was about 6'3". The guys dressed sharply and wore fedoras, and the two ladies were nice looking and smelled good. Angie was tall and curvy, and Mary was about my height and very pretty.

Footlong and his crew would go to Eddie and Larry's house during the day while their mother was at work, where they'd clean up and hang out for two or three hours. We often went over to see them and hear about what was going on in the streets and gambling houses. I was always talking the game I'd learned from running with the Sand Town crew and trying to act like I was up on stuff—like sex. Footlong and his friends would laugh, so I felt good about lying, but one day, they called my bluff. I didn't know it, but I was about to be initiated.

This particular day, Footlong took Eddie, Larry, Chris, and Mary to the store up the street, leaving me in the house with John and Angie. Angie said she was going into the bedroom to lie down for a minute.

After she did, John winked his eye at me and told me to go on in with her. I was scared and said that Footlong might kick my butt if I did. John said, "If you don't go in there and get on it, *I'm* going to kick your butt. You been talking big, so get on with it."

I went into the bedroom and saw that Angie was in the bed, naked beneath the sheets. I was more afraid of John than of her, so I undressed while Angie silently watched. Then I slipped between the sheets and lay next to her. As you can imagine, I was pretty excited, and while I won't go into details, I came out of that bedroom a well-educated young man. I was smiling and happy, but I was scared, too, because I didn't know what was going to happen next.

Footlong and the others came home, and we all sat around, eating and drinking. John and Angie laughed between themselves, and I was embarrassed and nervous, waiting for them to spill the beans. They never did let on, though. For the next couple of years, Angie occasionally had sex with me, but that stopped after John was killed in a car wreck.

As for me, my life was about to change again.

Chapter
5

Sports, Survival, and an Unexpected Journey

Survival during my teen and young adult years was difficult. The world was changing regarding race, especially with the passage of the Civil Rights Act in 1964. Yet while some things seemed to improve on the surface, the South's core philosophy of racism held steadfast. The more I learned, the less hope I had because I was beginning to understand the injustices and lies being taught to students in public schools. The American education system, the legal and judicial systems, and most Southern people, black as well as white, drilled one simple message into the Southern psyche: Black people were inferior humans compared to white people. Willie Lynch reigned supreme.

Even many Christian churches and civic organizations followed this code, and not surprisingly, I had serious issues with this mindset since it contradicted the word of God. God says that all people are of the same substance and are equal in his sight. Weren't black people made with the same or equal proportion of Godly care and ingredients as whites? It appeared that when discussing blacks, many white preachers did not think so or believe what the Bible says about brotherly love and the brotherhood of man. They seemed to view God as a respecter of human distinctions of color, race, wealth, and intellect. All good thing came to whites in the here and now, but nonwhites had to wait for the by-and-by, whatever that meant.

Black people were taught to believe and pray but also to struggle through the hardships of life and to accept with passive agreement whatever demands and burdens white people placed on them. Only white men could mingle with women of any race and reproduce. This had been going on since the beginning of our country, during three centuries of slavery in which white men had dehumanized black men while at the same time having sex with black women. The affair of one early American president with one of his black slaves went on in open view in the White House, and he even fathered several children by her.

I realized that people were not just lying but using fear and ignorance as weapons to control the hopes and dreams of minorities. The victims of this fraud did not know any better, and confusion and lack of understanding hindered people from finding a better way. Further, society offered very few success stories to serve as models for Southern blacks to emulate. I wanted to know why that was so, and I wanted justice and fair play. I believed that, at some level, individuals and groups of people within American society could and should see thing differently and treat everyone with respect, equality, and justice. I thought elected representatives, judges, and other officials should and would get things right.

But money and power corrupt. Fear and pride cloud the truth. Society as a whole said that Negroes were inferior and lacking as human beings. School books, religious leaders, and the people who enforced the legal system were complicit in the attitudes and behaviors that regulated the lives of Southern blacks, often supporting and reinforcing the status quo with what amounted to terrorism. I was even more discouraged than ever, for one thing was clear: as a Negro boy, I was nothing more than a member of a peculiar species of near-human beings. If society's leaders and nearly everyone else practiced Jim Crow, where could there be hope for someone like me? What could my dreams amount to but frustration? My mother often told me, "God makes a way where there is no way," but society told me I had very little value. All I could expect—all I *should* expect—was to accept hard menial labor, my place of servitude, and a belief in the rights and will of white people. Despite the Civil Rights Act, the American dream remained just a fantasy for Southern blacks.

As I learned more facts—or more important, that some "facts" are not facts at all—I also came to realize that tricksters and fakers, like that fifth-grade teacher with his football scam, were everywhere. I'd even been one of them when I was younger. The people I relied on to tell the truth were not being truthful. I did not know what to believe, but questions still rose in my mind of why people—blacks as well as whites—were so misled about the so-called physical and mental limitations of African Americans. But the subject wasn't easy to talk about. At that time, voicing questions or raising doubts about the validity of the situation could be physically and economically dangerous. Asking for human rights, due process, and equality from the justice system was viewed as bad conduct by black people.

You have to understand that this was a different time and a different generation. The black community was largely institutionalized with African Americans willing to maintain the status quo through the Willie Lynch system of segregation, subjugation, and self-indoctrination. Even so, some of the more progressive African Americans were beginning to stand up and speak out. Many who supported change were trying to figure out the best way to achieve it, and their methods ran from the pacifist marches led by Dr. Martin Luther King to the guns sported in public by the Black Panthers. To me, that latter behavior was way out there, and to my surprise, it was looked upon negatively not just by whites but by most blacks as well. But the bottom line was that both approaches made it obvious that African Americans were tired of oppression. They weren't going to take it any longer and were going to stand up for themselves.

That wasn't easy to do in those days. Anyone who did was labeled a radical and a troublemaker who might be potentially dangerous. But the cat was out of the bag. Blacks were beginning to show solidarity in their movement to achieve racial equality within society, and we'd never seen anything like that before. I didn't know if that was a good thing or a bad thing since it was all new ground.

Confused about all that was going on, I asked my teachers and coaches and the men at the barbershop what they thought about Malcom X, Dr. Martin Luther King, H. Rap Brown, Stokely Carmichael, Elijah Muhammad, Jesus, congressmen, and others. I wanted to know what was what and who was who, but the answers depended on whom

I talked to: a middle-class black business owner, a teacher, or a guy on the street. The more the person was entrenched in the prevailing socioeconomic state, the more traditional their answers would be because they felt like they were above others and were benefitting from the status quo. That made them take issue with radicals like Malcolm X, maybe because they felt that such people might threaten their own status.

But others were more sympathetic. I learned from them, for example, that Malcolm X was a complex man who wasn't afraid to change his beliefs and life strategies when faced with new information. He started out as Christian, then he became a Muslim who was stone-cold against whites. Finally, he evolved to view life from a standpoint of equality. What got him was that he found out that the Black Muslim faith being promoted in the United States was different from other branches of the Muslim religion. Here, Islam was being presented as a black religion. But Malcolm X discovered that Islam, just as with Christianity with its many different forms and sects, also is diverse in its followers and specific beliefs. Blacks in the US who turned to Islam weren't going to Mecca or reading Islamic texts, so they generally had no idea of who practiced Islam or what it was really about. But Malcolm X learned those things by traveling. Traveling allows one to see things for oneself, to meet others with different ideas, and to form opinions based on a larger set of facts and experiences.

In traveling and meeting leaders of various aspects of Islam, Malcolm X experienced Islam at its root as well as in many of its branches, giving him a broader perspective not just on Islam as a whole but also on the version being practiced in the Black Muslim community in the US. He discovered that Muslims around the world were a rainbow of human colors—white as well as the colors of all the other races—and to cap it off, he read the *hadith*, which is the narrative records of the customs and sayings of Muhammad and his companions. In this, he learned that Muhammad himself was a white man with black slaves who also promoted assassinations, sometimes because of beliefs, sometimes because of power struggles. That made Malcolm X look on Muhammad as man rather than a demigod. So when Malcolm X came back to the States, he began speaking in more conciliatory tones about whites and became critical of the Black Muslim movement and especially of Elijah Muhammad, the head of the Black Muslims in the US. He was excited about the truth, but he didn't know how to weigh that out before he started pointing fingers. In failing to understand diplomacy, he effectively signed his own death warrant.

So from the example of Malcolm X, I learned that if I was going to search for the truth, my life would be changed forever. I hoped that I wouldn't be killed because I knew that I could be easily eliminated and not even have a chance. But despite the implied danger, I knew I would have to seek the truth about society and myself. And gradually, over time, I began to grasp the issues and the players—enough that I could begin to form my own opinions of what was going on around me.

Some aspects of my life continued to advance despite the institutionalized racism all around me. Sports, of course, was paramount among my interests, and during high school, I was more positively influenced by my coaches than by anyone else. We had some really great people with progressive ideas, and that was good for me because I was coming of age and trying to figure out how to make it in life. So I was looking up to people who had intelligence, knowledge, and life experience to help me make the transition.

The standout on the coaching staff was head coach Ben Arthur Young, whom we just called Coach. He was a 5'10", 220-pound ex–college fullback who'd been born in the San Angelo, Texas, area. He'd attended Prairie View A&M University, one of the major black universities in Texas, and had served as the head football coach in Hillsboro, Texas, before coming to Carver High School. As the head football and track coach, he was well known in the area, but his fame rested more on his personality than on his position.

Amazingly, considering his position and influence, Coach had been blinded by diabetes by the time I got to high school. Despite that, he let his confidence, experience, and faith show him a way even when his eyes couldn't. In the early days, he didn't even use a cane. He was a little like the cartoon character Mr. Magoo. Most of the time, he'd just take off walking and make his way, though it wasn't always the right direction. At practice or during games, he'd sometimes head off the wrong way down the sideline, yelling, "Run that ball!"

We were always messing with him, sending him off in the wrong direction or chuckling when we saw him talking to thin air when he thought somebody was there. And often he'd have his foot in his mouth because kids would bait him to talk smack about people who were close enough to hear. And what he said was usually wild and crazy since he often took things to the extreme. That kind of baiting and razzing might have bothered Coach when he was younger, but by the time I knew him, he was pretty thick-skinned. One time, though, he and one of the assistant coaches got into a scuffle, and Coach was throwing punches that weren't landing because he couldn't see his opponent.

Coach was the master of communication—positive, negative, and in between. He spoke in a baritone crossed with a bulldog's rumble—the kind of voice that didn't need a microphone. Even better, his presentation skills were exceptional, and he often served as the MC, presenter, or play-by-play announcer for area events. People loved the way he sprinkled his talk with humorous analogies, such as "He's pitching aspirins today" for a pitcher whose throws are so fast, the batter can barely see them, or "That ball's got baking powder on it," meaning the ball is sailing on out of the stadium.

I'd already learned that the wrong kind of hustle was wrong for many reasons, but in Coach, I witnessed the right kind of hustle. He was not only an amazing man but a true hustler in the best sense, always working with sports and summer programs. He could engage with anyone, and his recall was extraordinary. And of course, he had to deal with typical complaints from everybody—students, parents, teachers, coaches, and administrators, alike—not to mention the jokes about his blindness, but I never saw or heard of him being down or discouraged. To the contrary, I often saw him encourage others with words, gifts, and resources.

Coach could be as tough as he was generous, and his manner earned him enemies as well as friends. He was challenged often, but he never showed weakness or sorrow. He might have lived in denial in one area or another, but he never submitted, and he gave as good as he received. I saw his good side and bad, and he came to like and encourage me. In turn, I was one of his supporters, and I best remember Coach as a mentor to me and many others.

One of Coach's teammates when he played football for Prairie View was Lester G. Broadus, who was my sixth-grade teacher as well as our defensive coach. Coach Broadus was from Denton, Texas, and was

6'2" and about 230 pounds. He'd played in the military in Germany and had been All-Conference when he played for Prairie View as a tight end. He'd coached in Cleveland, Texas, before coming to Carver, where he also coached baseball. He even won the baseball state championship in 1964, just prior to integration.

Another coach was Cleopus Bables. I think he was from West Texas. About 5'10" and 200 pounds, he was a science teacher and coached middle school basketball and football. An intelligent man, he was a great guy and a good conversationalist. He definitely had his own vision and opinions about life, and they were a little more progressive than those held by most of the other teachers at the time. You could say he was a bit of a radical, but that came out only in conversation, not in his actions. After Coach Young passed, Coach Bables took up some of his mantle as confidant and sounding board for students. Later, he became assistant athletic director for the Waco Independent School District.

One of many good things about my school was that the administration kept bringing in people with different ideas, like Coach Bables, along with those who were more conventional. These educators were interested in helping boost society to the next level, which was certainly not part of the status quo in the South. When African Americans came through with progressive thinking and asked to be treated equally, asserted themselves, or stood up as a leader outside their own community, a lot of people, including educators and religious leaders, were not supportive. After Bables became an administrator, his ideas shifted to become more in tune with social norms in order to maintain his position.

Our fifth-and sixth-grade health and PE teacher was Clarence Chase. He was from Mart, Texas, and he attended Paul Quinn College, where he played on the offensive line. Coach Chase was about an inch taller than Coach Broadus, but they weighed about the same. Dark skinned and handsome, he had a facility with words and verbal expressions to rival any experienced country preacher. While his demonstrations and speeches might have sometimes revealed the limits of his knowledge, he was a persuasive motivator of the imagination and the will to succeed.

Although there were no sports for girls at Carver, I should mention some of the women teachers who mentored and influenced hundreds of our students. I've already talked about Ms. Watson, our queen of etiquette, but there also was Ms. Johnson, our high school English teacher. She was an older lady who dressed and smelled nice and was our sunshine girl. The librarian, Ms. Forney, was very smart, polished, and articulate. Her daughter ended up going to Rice University, in Houston, a couple of years before I graduated. There also was a young lady who was a counselor for the band.

Overall, we Carver students were very fortunate in the quality of the educators we came in contact with, and they had a definite impact on most of us over the years. They were the most competitive group of people I'd been around, and through their example, they challenged us to be more competitive as well.

Friends and Relations

My best friend during high school was Scottie Reese. I'd known him since elementary school, but because he lived in a nearby neighborhood instead of the projects, we didn't become best friends until high school. By then, Scotty had developed into an extraordinary young man: tall, handsome, and athletic. He wasn't as blind as Coach, but he had to wear glasses that were thick as Coke-bottle bottoms. His father, who was ex-military, had a job at General Tire and Rubber Company, which was a big-time job in Waco. Scottie was in the middle of six children and was intelligent and quick with his tongue. His whole family was like that and always had a ready response to anything. Being a whiz at schoolwork, Scottie frequently helped me complete my assignments. He started playing football in his sophomore or junior year.

As is common in high school, I had a different girlfriend each year. High school romance is usually an ephemeral thing. A lot of times, girls were attracted to you or not depending on which sports were in season at the time. And younger guys, especially, view themselves as know-it-alls and protectors. I know that often was true for me, so my relationships weren't really about the girl or the relationship but about what I wanted. But then you might get tricked by your girl and suddenly realize how vulnerable you are.

That wasn't uncommon, and a lot of gaming went on regarding boyfriend-girlfriend relationships. Everybody was looking at somebody else on the side. Everybody was trying to be in the position of being in love, but then here came a new boy or a new girl, and all that love just got up and left, and you moved on to another person. Sometimes I fell in love, though never deeply, and nothing worked out for long. My relationships were more like friendships than anything else, which was good for me since I didn't have a lot of male friends. My longtime friend, James, had moved to San Antonio to live with his dad, and though there were a couple of guys, like Scotty, whom I associated with, most of the time, I just hung out with my current girlfriend.

Since my mother couldn't afford to buy clothes for me, I worked all summer every year of high school to save money to buy my own clothes. The summers of my fifteenth and sixteenth years, I worked at a brickyard making pallets and stacking raw bricks on them to prepare them for baking. That was very strenuous work. The summer I was seventeen, I worked as a janitor at the ALICO Building in Waco, which, at twenty-two stories, is still the tallest building in the city. I was the relief guy when regular workers went on vacation. My mom started letting me use the car a little bit to travel to and from work, but I didn't have much of a life. I'd just go to work and come home beat.

At the end of my senior year, I worked at Mrs. Baird's Bakery. That was one hard job—probably the toughest I ever had. You'd start at 2:00 or 3:00 am and work the rest of the night and into the morning. Those late hours made the job tough, especially on a young man. I'd have a late-night date with my girlfriend and then head off to the bakery afterward. The one thing I learned is that I never wanted to work in a bakery again. Baking is a hard job and a little dangerous, too, since you can get burned on the baking pans while you're trying to keep up with the production line. That added pressure and stress to an already strenuous situation.

As far as schoolwork went, I have to admit that I wasn't much interested in reading and writing, so I tended to do somewhat poorly in literary studies. Math was my strong point, but I paid attention in my other classes and had friends who'd help me out after school. Even though I wasn't an outstanding student, I did well enough to make the honor roll fairly often.

Part of my problem was that, as far as the faculty went, I didn't have a lot of support in high school. I was a very confused young man, and it's hard to forge bonds when you're an outsider. So I never found much of a connection with any of my teachers—not the way I could connect with my coaches. These men, who mentored hundreds of young men during their careers at Carver, were cool, gave me a great deal of support, and greatly influenced me. I took to hanging out with them when I wasn't in class or at practice, listening to their stories and gradually catching on to some things—not just about sports but about life in general.

I've already related how I got into sports midway through my last year of middle school. My high school sports career started with track and basketball, and when football season rolled around, I was introduced to organized football. It was quite different from any other sport I'd played, partly because it was varsity football, and some of the guys I was playing with were three or four years older than I was, so it was a tremendous change, not to mention a challenge. But it was my opportunity to try to accomplish something for myself and to see if I had any skills.

I chose sports for a couple of reasons, one being that it definitely helped make me somebody on campus. But I also was trying to figure a way out of being trapped by society in a role I didn't want. Sports was a way of using my time productively, and I wasn't alone in this sort of effort. Sports was one of the few avenues that African Americans could use to rise in society. Plus, we were looking for any kind of way to feel good about ourselves, and sports offered not only that but also a means to extend positive influence outside the self. Even if you didn't go to college, you were looked on favorably in your own community, and that could lead to better things, such as a good job and higher social standing. And if you were great enough, your reputation and influence could even become international in scope. There was no limit to what you could accomplish depending on your ability and drive.

There are pitfalls, however, to almost any situation, sports included. Track is really the major sport in which a competitor has a chance to excel individually on his or her own abilities and merits. The situation is much different in team sports, especially at levels higher than high school, where you need an atmosphere of cooperation, the other players' appreciation, and all the other factors that go along with operating as a team. But that sort of cooperation is often difficult to achieve. In pro sports back then, most of the black players ended up stacked one behind the other, each competing against all the others for that one good position. Situations like that can lead to rivalries, resentments, internal strife, and all the other sorts of situations that can derail a young kid depending on his or her ability to recognize and deal with conflict.

Even so, sports was one of the best shots a young black man had to rise in society, though if you wanted to try for it, you had to work hard. A lot of kids thought they had that kind of work ethic, but many didn't. Consequently, their opportunities were even less than average in America. Life was tough in all respects. When you're young, you tend to believe your parents, other adults, and books because they're the ones who are supposed to know and guide you into life. If they're all telling you that you're a lesser form of human, it's hard to rise above that.

Just as bad, there are black people who are inspired and motivated by white society and who preach the same thing, whether it's because they are institutionalized or bought and paid for. And you discover that you become the enemy of everybody if you think differently, if you view yourself as better than you're told you are, or if you behave in ways unacceptable to the white-dominant society—in short, if you're not playing the right role. So the expectation I had growing up was to put myself last. It was crazy. Even though I knew I wasn't the best athlete or the best student, I recognized that all this was crazy. But I also understood that if you want to rise, you can't feel sorry for yourself, even if your opportunities are limited because of your skin color or other factors.

Trials, Tribulations, and College Prospects

These thoughts became paramount when, at the end of my junior year, my mom asked me what was I going to do after I graduated the next year. At first, I didn't understand her meaning, so she clarified by saying, "Well, you're going to have to find yourself somewhere to go. To live. To grow up. To be a man. To make something of yourself."

It dawned on me that she was exactly right. I needed to make plans. I'd already been thinking about college, but her words made me focus those thoughts in a practical way. If I was going to even consider going to a university, I knew I'd have to work on getting a scholarship. So my senior year was all about sports and academics. I began paying closer attention to my schoolwork so I could keep up my grades, and I worked out a lot and played basketball, football, and baseball. In track and field, I threw the discus and was a backup runner. I was out of the band, but I sang a pretty good first bass in an a cappella group and in our excellent school choir. I also was on the student council. I was doing everything I could to go to college. I could have joined the ROTC and become an officer, but the Vietnam War was going on at the time, and the ROTC guys had to go to Vietnam. Nobody wanted that. At least I didn't.

I took a test that is given every year by the Negro Scholarship Fund. If you scored well, they'd help support you in getting into a historically black colleges or university, and you could even receive a scholarship. I scored well, but I never did pursue their scholarship offer because eventually a better opportunity opened up for me. More on that later, but at the time, the thought was that I might be able to get a scholarship to go to Howard University or some other traditionally black college outside Texas. I was looking at those things and trying to figure out what would be best and who would offer me something, all the while feeling kind of desperate.

That's what was on my mind as well as trying to juggle the whole school thing and hoping that some recruiter would notice my athletic skills. I admit that I wasn't studying as hard as I could have, mostly because I had friends and girlfriends who helped me, and I just accepted their help. But I still had to put out a lot of effort because of all the time involved in homework. Sometimes that frustrated me because it was material that I had to memorize even if I was never going to need it again. Math and reading and writing, however, were extremely important since those were what you were being tested on in the SAT.

Unfortunately, I'd never done a lot of reading and writing, so those were my weakest areas and really hurt me when I took the

SAT and other tests. I always did better in math because in that you just have to understand the terminology and the factors that you're working with and follow the formulas to get to the answers. In reading comprehension, though, teachers used terms I'd never heard before, and that limited my understanding of what they were talking about, which lowered my scores. You can't answer a question when you don't understand the terms of the question. Basically, that was disheartening and stemmed from the fact that I hadn't really felt challenged in high school to do all that much work as long as I was able to skate along on what I could memorize or figure out. It wasn't that I couldn't do the work; I'd just never done it in a way that made the material really sink in.

In fact, it was impossible to do everything that our teachers were asking of us. We had hours of homework on top of remembering this theme, that epic, or those ideas. Our teachers were very good and talented people, but they also were driven, and they drove us too. And on top of that were sports and extracurricular activities. In the end, there simply wasn't enough time to do everything that was being asked of us, so we had to pick and choose which areas we were going to concentrate on.

School wasn't all hard work, and I did find ways to express myself, even if it was unexpected. One funny thing happened in my senior year. Every so often, the school would have a talent show where the students could demonstrate their special abilities, and when the Christmas show rolled around, I decided to participate. I was billed to sing "Your Precious Love" by Marvin Gaye and Tammi Terrell, which was a huge Motown hit that all the girls loved, but I'd made secret plans with my choir teacher, who was playing accompaniment on piano. After I stepped onto the stage, she started in on the opening bars of "Your Precious Love," and all the girls sat up expectantly. Then she suddenly changed the tune, and I burst out in the Frank Sinatra song "Strangers in the Night." I sang it pretty well, but my singing a Sinatra song caused the audience to burst out in laughter. Everybody usually took me for a very serious person, so for me to do something off the wall like that really tickled them. I picked the Sinatra song because it matched my vocal range, which was not "strong Frank" but close enough.

As my decision about college approached, I had to face an issue that was rising in the black community. Before this time, blacks who wanted to go to college had been limited to historically black colleges and universities like Paul Quinn College in Waco, Prairie View A&M, Bishop College in Dallas, or Grambling State University in Louisiana. Most of these schools were not state supported but were affiliated with religious institutions. A handful of major universities might be available to the ambitious, such as the University of Washington, Notre Dame, the Navy Academy, and the University of Colorado, which already had recruited several kids from A. J. Moore High School, the other black high school in Waco. Moore High was very competitive athletically and put out a lot of athletes who went pro. In general, though, neither black students looking for a college nor their counselors were thinking that big at the time. Most of my counselors and peers thought that the most important thing was to find a black college somewhere and go to it because otherwise, the Vietnam War beckoned. So at first, I was steered toward black colleges in Texas.

But the world was changing. With desegregation, state-run universities also began admitting black students, and suddenly, my opportunities were wider than had traditionally been the case. My best friend, Scottie, got a scholarship to attend Marshall University, and even before my SAT scores came back, I began receiving letters from several larger state universities that were integrated but were primarily white. Notable among them was Wichita State University, which offered me a scholarship and an opportunity to play football. I also received letters from other universities, such as the University of Colorado, the University of Southern California, and Purdue, and I visited a couple of the closer ones, like East Texas State. I started thinking, *Wow, is this possible? Can I go to USC or Purdue or the University of Colorado?* The prospect encouraged me to consider a broader scope than Prairie View and other black colleges in Texas. The main problem I had in doing that was that I didn't know any adults—teachers and coaches included—who'd gone to any of these other colleges. The lack of a trailblazer to show me a clear path made it difficult to get an idea of what any of these universities might be like, what they had to offer, and how I might fare there.

Then something happened that I could not, in my wildest dreams, have anticipated. In late January or early February, Jake Hess and Gilbert Bartosh, two coaches from Rice University in Houston, drove up to Waco to scout for football players, including Michael Tyler, who was a running back for Waco High School. Rice, for those who don't know, is a small private university and one of the finest schools in the South, consistently ranking in the top twenty universities in the country.

Hess and Bartosh viewed a film of a Waco High game to see how Mike played. They liked what they saw, then they watched a film of a different game to check out another player from a town south of Dallas. It so happened that this player's team was playing Carver, and when Hess and Bartosh saw me play, they grew interested. Later, they came by Carver to check out my academic record, test scores, character, and so forth to see if I might qualify to attend Rice, which maintains very strict academic standards, even for athletes. I didn't get to meet them, but to my amazement—and even before my SAT scores came in—they showed interest in me, though they did wait a week or two before inviting me to Houston to visit the university.

The fact that I was being recruited by Rice blew everyone's minds at school, including my coaches'. Nobody there thought that I would ever go to a school such as Rice. I certainly didn't. And that attitude extended to my neighbors in the projects. They couldn't believe that the son of Eunice, the maid, was going to Rice. After all, I wasn't the greatest student. They all figured that even if I got in, I'd be back home after the first semester. Everyone wondered why I'd want to take a chance on going to a ritzy, predominantly white private school when I could have gone to Prairie View or somewhere else where I might be more accepted and successful.

Almost overnight, a lot of negativity built up toward me—it was that old crabs-in-the-bucket thing. But I occasionally found relief from the pressure. One day, Coach Bables approached me in the gym and asked, "What do you think about going to school? Who are you talking to?" I told him that several schools had contacted me, and he said, "I heard that Rice is interested." I said, "They are, but I don't know too much about them," and he said, "Well, shoot, that's a no-brainer."

"What do you mean?" I asked, and he said, "You can't do better than going to Rice."

And I said, "Rice? I'm not a genius or anything," but he told me, "You're smart enough. You need to go to Rice."

His faith in my abilities definitely jazzed me up. I understood that Coach Bables wasn't saying that I was the smartest kid, but he knew that I was intelligent, even if I didn't always use my smarts to the best advantage academically. What he was telling me was to live up to the challenge and that a Rice education and the opportunities that might follow were something I could go for and attain. It was the kind of encouragement I needed to hear because at that time in society, many young black men were trying to show their value to white society. We wanted to demonstrate that we were capable and productive, and here was Coach Bables, telling me that I was exactly those things. His words emboldened me, but I admit I was a little intimidated, too, because I knew I'd have to study hard, and I'd never really dedicated myself to schoolwork. But that was something I'd have to do if I considered going to Rice University.

A scout came to Waco and drove me to Houston along with Mike Tyler. Rice is a small but impressive school, and it has so much class and prestige that I was already sold on it before the visit. But if I hadn't been, the view we saw the moment we turned off of South Main and drove through the front gates would have nailed the deal. In front of us was a long, straight lane between rows of overarching oaks. Framed in the opening at the end of the lane was the university's main administration building, Lovett Hall, with its huge archway called the Sallyport. It was a spectacular view, and I was instantly hooked.

Mike and I soon met our recruiters: Tommy Alexander for me and Bucky Allshouse for Mike. Throughout the weekend of getting to know Rice and Rice getting to know us, Tommy and Bucky were always there for Mike and me. Their personalities, openness, and generosity showed us something that I'd never experienced before from white society. I'd grown up in an all-black culture, and there wasn't a lot of intermingling with white people. The only whites I'd personally dealt with were guys my own age, mostly on the football field. But on that trip to Rice, we socialized, we went out, we partied, and I got to see how genuine Tommy and Bucky were. I was really impressed with them. Not only were they smart, but they also were nice guys and had big hearts. Their openness toward Mike and me was instrumental in cementing my desire to attend the university they represented. To this day, I remain friends with both of them.

I knew that Rice would be tough and I'd have to do my best to meet the many challenges—academic, athletic, and social—not the least of which would be attending a college where I would be one of only a dozen black students on campus. It would be a major commitment on my part as well as the university's, and I knew that I'd have very little support—financial, social, or personal. Today, Rice is well known for supporting student needs, but that wasn't the case at that time. Back then, you had to find your own support system, and I didn't have one. But I decided I'd have to be okay with that and everything else, including the difficulties and trials.

I soon learned that the athletic facilities weren't much. The weight room was about the size of a bedroom. Rice is a small school and was even smaller back then—about 2,500 undergraduates—and it didn't generously finance the athletic program. Although there weren't exercise rooms or the other amenities you might find at some larger state schools, I remained very impressed with the university and appreciative of being offered the challenge of attending such a prestigious school. Even better, most of the people I met seemed receptive of me and the fact that I was black. Their lack of racial hostility in itself made the place attractive, but the real question was, Could I survive academically?

Since the results of my SAT hadn't yet come back, Rice gave me the test again. They could evaluate the scores right away. I took the test on Saturday, and the next day, right before we were about to go back to Waco, they called in the prospective players, one by one. I went in on Sunday morning, and they told me that my scores weren't high enough to qualify for the university but that the low test scores were the only reason I hadn't been accepted.

I was devastated. A fantastic opportunity for my future had evaporated right before my eyes. To lock it in, the SAT scores from the test I'd taken at Carver came back, and they were the same as those I'd received at Rice. It seemed I'd have to lay to rest any hope of going to Rice, so there was nothing to do but keep on exploring other schools. East Texas State still wanted me, and Colorado State University, among others, also expressed interest, but the offer of a scholarship made Wichita State the most attractive choice, and I leaned strongly in that direction.

It was a tense time because I didn't know where to go and what to do. The more I looked at other schools, the more my disappointment at not being accepted by Rice wore at me, and that disappointment woke me to the fact that I really wanted to go there. But I'd been told that was out, and when you're young and naive, you often hear older people say things, and you believe them 100 percent because they are coming from supposed authorities. When it comes to facing roadblocks, however, I've often been obstinate, no matter who says what. Maybe I got a little of that from Coach Young. And Coach Bables's words of encouragement rang in my head, stoking the fire that was already building in me to go to Rice. I knew I'd have to make a play for it once more.

So I did what I could to prepare to take the SAT once more. I slowed down and studied hard. I also spent a lot of time with God, trying to figure out if this was what he wanted me to do and asking him for guidance. Then I took the SAT a third time, concentrating to my fullest, even on the hardest parts. You can imagine how on edge I was, waiting for those new scores. Maybe it was the studying, maybe the prayers, or maybe it was a combination, but whatever the reason, my efforts miraculously paid off. The school counselor called me in and said, "How did you do that?"

I asked, "What are you talking about?" and he said, "The SAT. You improved your score by 200 points. How did you do that?"

I said, "I just prayed and did my best."

He said, "Well, your best and prayers got you passed, and your scores are high enough to get into Rice."

I called Rice to notify them, but to my surprise, they seemed a little casual and just said, "We'll get back to you." I was taken aback. In my naivete, I thought they really wanted me and they'd be so happy I'd qualified that admission would be automatic. In the interim, Baylor University called to tell me that they couldn't offer me a scholarship, but they'd be disappointed if I didn't go to Baylor and try out for their football team. While I would have liked being a Baylor Bear, I wasn't happy about their lack of a scholarship offer. For about a week, I was in limbo, torn between several okay-but-not-spectacular opportunities. I'd just about made up my mind to attend Wichita State when suddenly everything fell into place. Rice got back to me with the offer of a scholarship, and bam, my whole world changed almost instantly in every respect.

Jake Hess drove up to Waco, and Coach Young invited me and Mom to his house to sign the contract. That happened around the end of the first week in April, and suddenly I was officially a Rice Owl—and one of the first three African Americans to play football for Rice. That didn't stop the offers from other universities, though. Two weeks later, while I was at the regional track meet that was the prelude to the state playoffs, a guy from Texas Christian University came up and offered me a scholarship, but I had to tell him it was too late. I'd already signed with Rice.

When I was accepted by Rice, it blew everybody's minds. Mom was overwhelmed. She was very happy and proud, and the more she found out about Rice, the more proud she became. My mom was one of those ladies who has natural class even if she never had the chance to be classy. Instead, she'd lived a life of limited opportunities and economic status. So my being accepted to Rice was very important to her and gave her a chance to feel good about herself. Not only was I going to college, but I also was going to one of the best schools in the South.

But while my mom was proud of my achievement, being accepted by Rice presented problems at that I hadn't anticipated, though maybe I should have. During the last part of my senior year, I found myself fighting off teachers and principals who were trying to make me look bad and lose the Rice scholarship I'd just gotten. It was that crabs-in-a-bucket thing, and they were trying to pull me back in as I tried to climb out. Some of it was jealousy since I was getting a better scholarship than their own kids, and some of it was that my opportunity had been so unexpected, leaving everybody wondering how I'd done it. I even had two or three teachers and some front office personnel trying to get me kicked out of school. It was as if they were doing everything they could do to thwart me.

One of the worst offenders was my choir teacher, who became extra critical of me. My problems with her came to a head after a concert we performed five or six weeks out from graduation. It was a district-wide competition, and we sang really well, but soon after, the teacher told me I was no longer needed. She also said she was going to give me a zero on my test and a zero for my grade. I firmly believe that she was trying to jeopardize my Rice scholarship. It was disappointing to see adults act like that toward a child who was trying to better himself.

All through this time, Madea's support was crucial. When she saw all the negativity coming at me in school and everywhere else, she immediately understood the nature of the attacks. Mom also knew that I was just trying to lift myself up, so she got involved in the dispute with the choir teacher. She spoke with the principal about the situation, but unfortunately, the principal supported the choir teacher. Then Mom actually went to the school district superintendent to help straighten things out. In the end, it was resolved, and even though the bad test scores negatively affected my grade point average, Rice stuck to its guns, and my admission wasn't jeopardized. Together, Mom and I weathered the storm of animosity that seemed to swirl everywhere around me.

That was just part of what you had to deal with in a racially charged society in which black and white folks were always in a state of contention. Blacks weren't expected to do well, and whites didn't have any concept of blacks trying to break out of that mold. And a lot of your peers didn't want to see you come up from nothing and grow into something better. It seemed like it hurt them or something, and they often acted against the interests of blacks trying to rise. You expect that sort of jealous reaction from other kids, but I saw a lot of dirty stuff coming from adults as well, and that surprised me. I realized I'd just have to put up with it for the moment, and I hoped that things would be different once I got to college and afterward, if things worked out, moved on to the pros.

But the situation didn't get any better, only worse. As I went through each level and planned out my life, I had no idea that people too often behave like this. It seems that the higher you climb, the more that people want to pull you down. And then if you do fall down, the people who are your friends suddenly don't know you anymore. They'll cross the street to avoid meeting you on the sidewalk. Experiencing all those many negativities was far worse than hearing about them. Sometimes the aggression was blatant, sometimes more subtle, but in each case, I was shocked and surprised because, under the constant assault, all the things I was struggling to attain sometimes didn't seem real. But I'm getting ahead of myself. When I was a high school senior, being accepted by Rice wasn't something I was about to turn my back on.

It's a testament to the teachers and administration of Carver that about 70 percent of my class went to college. I graduated high school with 3A Second Team All-State Honors in football, was a state finalist in track, and had a scholarship in hand to attend one of the finest universities in the country. Changes in society and laws regarding racial equality, my high school successes, and my acceptance by Rice all came about in the span of just a few years and helped me survive. With where my head was at and what I was thinking, I couldn't have survived for long if the world had remained as it was when I was a child.

Graduation from high school was a mere formality. My high school was tired of me and ready to be rid of me, and I felt the same about the school. The situation outside school wasn't much better. As far as support went, I didn't have much. I had a couple of friends and a girlfriend I was into, but once I was accepted to college, everything that I'd had in high school just evaporated. I spent that whole summer on hold, just waiting to go to Rice, and nothing else in my life went anywhere. Even my relationship with my girl suffered and ended. Everybody was just waiting for me to leave, and I was ready to go because there was nothing in Waco to hold me.

That was the summer I worked at Mrs. Baird's Bread to make a little money. I think that Baird was a Rice graduate or something, and so they gave me a job. And I worked out to keep in shape. That was pretty much my summer, and while I bided my time, I brooded on how I was going to keep up academically at Rice since I reasoned that I would be at the bottom of my class due to my limited academic experience. I also worried about Rice society. How would I fare in this university that was almost all white and had a total of only twelve African American students? If it was any consolation, three of us were from Waco. But how were the people at Rice going to react and treat me? Were the professors going to be fair and friendly? Was I going to get any help since there was a whole lot I didn't know?

All those why and how questions that had been a part of my life growing up resurfaced with a vengeance, and the more I thought about it all, the more the pressure built. But it helped that I believed everything was happening for a reason. I knew I was going places I'd never been to experience things I didn't have any idea about, but I also knew that I was ready and willing.

Then the middle of August came, and it was time for me to make the move. Mom loaned me her car for a couple of weeks, and I loaded it up with my few possessions and drove to Houston. Before I left, I bought some clothes, and Mom gave me $20, saying, "Baby, this is all I got." But I had something better than her money. I had her love, best wishes, and encouragement, which were what I really needed. So I drove down to Houston and the Rice campus and unloaded my few possessions.

I'm here, I thought, pride mixing with trepidation. *I'm really a Rice Owl.*

Part Two
The Rice Owls

CHAPTER

6

A RICE OWL

Rice University had seemed like a dream, but now that it was real, I couldn't help but wonder what that reality would bring. I'd come from an essentially all-black society in Waco, only to be suddenly thrown into a mostly white society at Rice. Being a private school in the upper echelons of American universities, Rice had a social environment that was very different from anything I'd known. Not only was the territory unfamiliar, but so was the mindset I had to adopt. Everything about my life had abruptly changed to such a degree that it wasn't just new and different, it was surreal.

Luckily, I had a short buffer period to help me adjust since football players came in during the middle of August, two weeks earlier than the rest of the students. That meant that my first real contact with the university was through the coaches and my teammates.

Bo Hagan was the Owls' head coach. He'd played football and baseball, mostly for college teams, and coached football at the Georgia Institute of Technology and Southern Methodist University before being hired by famed Rice coach Jess Neely to serve as Rice's backfield coach. He worked under Neely for eleven years until he succeeded Neely as the Owls' head coach after the 1966 season. Coach Hagan was handsome, classy, and sociable, and he dressed well. He was always upbeat and encouraging, and I thought he was a good guy.

It's no secret that Hagan's coaching record at Rice wasn't on the same level as Neely's, but truthfully, he inherited some coaches and an athletic director who didn't back him. Maybe they thought he wasn't a "Rice guy," but whatever the reason, as far as I could tell, he was let down by a lot of the people working for him. Nor did they have the kind of egalitarian attitude he held toward other racial groups.

Another factor that inhibited Hagan was that the academic side of Rice was at war with athletics. The academics felt that sports were a waste of time and money and had no place at a school like Rice, and they were trying to eliminate the athletic programs. The attacks were vicious, and though the academics didn't succeed in shutting down athletics, their efforts hindered Hagan as much as anything else since he was fighting on that front as well as with his own athletic director, his staff, and our opponents on the field.

My freshman coach was Harold Mayo. He was a hard-nosed little guy, and while he was okay in some ways, he had that little-guy syndrome. Also, the only things he knew were what he already knew, and he wasn't a progressive thinker at all. He'd come to Rice just that year, and he probably got the job because a couple of his athletes had been recruited by Rice. He also had another syndrome that I saw played out time and again, not only in college but also later in the pros: he already had set in his mind which players he would try to promote, no matter how well—or poorly—they actually did on the field and despite the fact that other players might be playing better. He was that type of guy.

I learned over time and under different coaches that whether I started or not depended on a lot of factors: who the head coach wanted to develop the most, politics, and so forth. All those figured into who got to start and who got to play, but when you get down to it, all coaches like to win, and if you help them do that, it doesn't matter how redneck or prejudiced they are—you're their boy, at least for that week. And if you can go in there and show them what you have and that you can help them win, then you're going to get more playing time. So I wasn't particularly worried about Mayo or the other coaches. I was there to perform and win, and I thought that if I did that, I wouldn't have any problems, and things would work out in the end.

My new environment and the hard work we were doing in training pretty much occupied my time and energies those first two weeks. The freshman students among us took organized tours of the university and started practicing and mingling with our older teammates. Even the latter was novel since all but three of us—Mike Tyler, Stahlé Vincent, and myself—were white. Though I'd competed with white players on the field during my senior year of high school, I'd never had white teammates. Now, when I looked around the locker room, it seemed like all I saw was white faces. That was definitely odd. Until now, I hadn't generally thought of myself as black unless it was called to my attention. I was just myself, looking out on the world and interacting with it. Plus, I'd come from an environment where people weren't described by their color since everyone around me was black. Now I saw that I'd have to distinguish.

The dormitories at Rice are referred to as "residential colleges." Each residential college houses a cross section of the student population, and students are generally associated with the same college for their entire time as a Rice undergraduate. But I'm going to continue to refer to the colleges as dormitories since that's the more common term. When the team first arrived at Rice ahead of the rest of the students, we were housed in a really nice, brand-new dorm, though it was just a temporary arrangement. Once the other students arrived, we'd be assigned to a permanent dorm with a fresh set of roommates.

After the majority of students arrived, things got even more interesting as I met and mingled with a lot of people from all over the country and even outside it. Most were nice, if not overly friendly. It's true that some of the white kids didn't seem inclined to say anything to any of the African Americans. If they didn't like blacks, they just didn't talk to you. But others were curious about us black students and were happy to mingle and carry on conversations. It might not have been that they liked you, but that they wanted to learn something about you on a personal level, such as who you were, where you came from, and what you came to the university to accomplish. Remember, all this was taking place just four years after desegregation. Though some of the white students knew something about black culture based on prior associations with African Americans, many of them hadn't been in an integrated environment before either. Whites might have been the dominant group, but the situation was still a little like East meets West.

Rice freshman were called "weenies" by the other students, and weenies resided at the bottom of the Rice student hierarchy. As a weenie, I was assigned one of the shabbier rooms in Weiss College, which was a definite let-down. It was one of the oldest dorms on campus, and by the time I lived there, it was in pretty raggedy condition. It was built like a motel, with each room opening onto the outside instead of onto a hallway, and worse, the building was so old that it didn't have air-conditioning. Instead, they had water coolers in each room, but the coolers constantly broke down, so if it was hot, too bad for you. I couldn't help but wonder what was going on here. This was Rice University, and they couldn't afford to fix the air conditioners and heaters? Well, the university had the money; they just didn't want to spend it on an old building they intended to replace. That old building has since been demolished, and a newer facility was built there. But at least the bed was seven feet long—large enough to accommodate big people.

Mike Tyler was my roommate. He was a nice, handsome guy with a little mustache and beard, and we got along well. We spent a lot of time talking, and he was encouraging in his outlook. Mike was very conscious about how he looked. I'm not going to say he was vain, but he could spend two hours with scissors and comb in front of a mirror, clipping and snipping and making himself look pretty. And that's not counting the time it took him to get dressed, which he always did perfectly, from head to toe. Anytime we planned to go somewhere in the evening, he'd have to start getting ready in late afternoon.

All that preparation sometimes backfired on Mike. One afternoon, he, Stahlé, and I decided to go to a club located on Almeda Road, about a mile away on the other side of Hermann Park and the golf course from Rice. So we put on our nice clothes and shoes, which, of course, took Mike three hours. Then, looking sharp, we set out. We didn't have a car, but it wasn't far, so even though it was night, we walked. What we didn't take into account was that back then, there was a horse-riding stable on the edge of the park, and we ended up walking through a field where the horses had left a lot of droppings. By the time we got to the club, our shoes looked like—well, they looked pretty bad, so we went around the side of the building and did our best to clean them off. Then we went into the club and had a good time. Afterward, of course, none of us had enough money for a cab, so off we went trudging back across the horse pasture. By the time we got back to the dorm, we looked like hillbillies.

Rice students were known for their "jacks," or practical jokes, and I guess my room got jacked so much because it was on the end of the building and an easy target. Sometimes students messed with the air cooler to needle us for one reason or another. Other times, they'd pour some foul-smelling stuff on the cooler or door, making the room stink for weeks. And then there were the water balloons. I might come out of my room and get hit with two or three. Some of those guys would sit up all night just to get the chance to ambush you. One morning, I opened the door and started to stretch, and there's this guy waiting out there. He splashed me with a balloon right to the chest then ran for his dorm. I took off after him, caught up, and tackled him. That's what football players do, right? But what was I going to do then? I couldn't get physical, or I'd get kicked out of school, so all I could do was tell him to quit doing that.

Another bad thing, especially for athletes who need regular meals, was that the cafeteria didn't serve dinner on either Saturday or Sunday, and if you were a poor student athlete like I was, that meant you sometimes went hungry, especially if you missed breakfast or lunch. On those days, you'd find yourself wandering around the dorm, checking out your friends to see if they had anything to eat.

If being in close proximity to whites in the locker room was strange, stranger still was living with whites. I thought I knew about white people, but I found out I didn't really know all that much. And they didn't know a lot of things about black people, either. The separation of the races had led to estrangements between them on many levels, and most folks on both sides only saw the stereotypes, not the people themselves. So a lot of the ideas that people based their actions on just weren't true, and our mingling was unfamiliar territory for all of us. But any trepidation I might have felt at showering and living with teammates and roommates of different races pretty much disappeared during the first couple of days. After that, I didn't think much about that aspect.

The only times racial differences came up was during conversations in which "black" and "white" were used to describe people being talked about. Stories often pivoted on whether the subject of the story was black or white, though sometimes that description wasn't overt, and it took the events of the story to reveal the subject's race. I don't know if mentioning race was merely description or if it had any special significance for any of my white acquaintances. For me, the description might have helped broadly characterize the subject of the story, but the way a person spoke about race when telling a story definitely lent me a broader understanding of the personal character of the storyteller.

Through my interactions with white teammates, I gained an increasing understanding of the relevance of race among whites of my own age group, within the university, and within society as a whole. Even when routine made the atmosphere in a room amenable, the question of race always hung in the air. Whatever the bottom line might have been, though, we all listened to one another's stories. They were amazed by some of the stories I had to tell, and I was surprised by some of theirs. It was an open exchange, and though it was a new sort of situation for all of us, there wasn't any combativeness at all—except on the playing field. There, it was all competition. But off the field, socialization didn't entail a lot of pileups as we learned about one another.

I often visited other students in their rooms to listen to their music and have long conversations about ourselves and our cultures. Generally, I was treated well, and I enjoyed it, but this was still the South. While most of the students tried to be nice and supportive, there were those who downright called you a nigger. Some of them knew that was a negative term and used it as a deliberate insult, but for others, the term was just another descriptive word because that's what they called black people back home. It was, in many ways, an unconscious prejudice.

I knew I couldn't control what other people thought or said. I'd learned that from all the bad-mouthing and negative reactions I'd gotten during my last year of high school. All I really could do was decide how to let that kind of thing affect me and how to respond. Was I going to take it and try to understand it, or was I going to get upset and mad? The situation was something I'd had no experience with—

nor did I have anyone to talk to about it—but I knew I was going to have to face it, one way or another.

And face it I did during my first week, when this white guy came up to me and said, "Hey, nigger. Where you from?" and that sort of thing. I was caught off guard even though I'd known it was bound to happen. And here it was. He had a big smile on his face, as if implying that what he'd said was okay and normal.

I said, "Hey, man, why you calling me a nigger?" and he replied, "Where I come from, we call all black people niggers."

I told him, "Oh no. I don't identify myself like that." We talked for a minute, and he listened to what I had to say, then we went on about our business. I was amazed at that sort of mindset, but the thing was, it was all new to me. This guy lived in the same dorm as I did, so I saw him from time to time, but we never associated. Maybe he didn't like me after that first conversation, and truthfully, I didn't have any fondness for him either. But we respected each other, and I think we both grew from that exchange.

Girls presented a whole other issue—especially white girls. Where I came from, if you were a black guy, you ran from white women as fast as you could. So associating with some of the white girls who were trying to be friendly, nice, and cool was really different. And that brought in a few of the redneck white boys who'd never seen a white girl talk to a black guy. They'd just stand there, staring and saying, "What's this?" The situation was new for everybody, and even the white students were under a lot of pressure to communicate and adjust to the sudden incursion of black students among them. All of us discovered that we had a lot of adjustments to make in feeling out personal and racial boundaries and that we had to find new ways of communicating with each other. It was sometimes difficult, yet through those times and trials, many of us continued to grow.

But racism isn't always overt and can take subtle forms. A good example is when one of the assistant coaches noticed that I was friends with this white girl. We weren't dating or anything, but anytime people saw black guys talking to white girls, it was an occasion for suspicion. This coach couldn't tell me not to associate with her because she was white and I was black, so he told me that she was a hussy whom I ought to stay away from.

"Surely you're better than that," he told me. The reality, though, was that she was nothing of the sort. The coach was just trying to find some supposedly legitimate reason for me not to be friendly with a white girl, but to do that, he had to resort to slandering her to put me in my place and keep me away from her. In essence, he was pitting one minority against another. That's what would happen most of the times when you had those sorts of incidents. They felt they had to put us down, but they couldn't directly attack us for being African Americans, so they'd shift the blame to somebody else but include us in any prohibitions that ensued.

When I left his office, I couldn't keep myself from bursting out laughing. In the first place, the coach was trying to steer me away from this girl by claiming she was a hussy, but I guess he didn't have much of a grip on the reality of the situation. I was a young guy, and hussies are exactly what young guys are looking for. And second was the irony of telling a black kid from the projects that somebody is beneath him. I laughed all the way back to the dorm, thinking of how the coach had put both of his feet in his mouth at the same time.

That coach's attempts to put me in my place didn't work too well, but parents often intervened where the coach failed. A good example is this other white girl I dated for a short time while I was a sophomore. We liked each other, and one time, she invited me to dinner at her parents' house. I was looking forward to a home-cooked meal, but dinner was terrible. My date's mom had tried to cook a fillet of sole, but she put too much vinegar on it, and I just couldn't eat it, though I did manage to eat the vegetables. After dinner, we sat around talking. My date had a younger sister who was a whiz in medieval history, so there went Mom, siccing little sister on me to check out my intelligence by grilling me in medieval history. She'd ask the younger daughter a question about the subject, and the girl would say what she thought, and then the mom would turn to me and ask, "Well, what do you think about it, Rod?" I'm sure she was trying to embarrass me and make me look bad in front of her daughters, but it so happened that I was taking medieval history that very semester, and I remembered enough to satisfy her. And all the time, my date's father was sitting right there at the head of the table, observing and judging. I thought that the whole episode was pretty lame. I was the guest, and instead of trying to intimidate me or see how much I knew about her culture, the mom should have asked me more about where I came from. But she and Dad didn't care where I came from. They were only concerned about where their daughter was going, and they quickly sent her to Paris. In fact, enforced separation seemed to be the standard operating procedure utilized by a lot of parents, and the two or three other white girls who invited me to dinner at their homes also were packed off to school in Europe. They'd call me up crying and telling me that Mommy and Daddy were sending them away. You could practically hear the parents in the background going, "No, no, no. No way."

The freshman class had only six or seven hundred students, and we'd have these parties—mixers—each weekend to have some kind of socialization amid the tremendous pressures Rice put on everyone to be academically successful. This was my first real chance to mingle with the full range of other students, and basically, I went just to look around and meet people. But in the end, the experiences I gained and lessons I learned were valuable. Let me put it in terms of music. I'd come from a culture where black music—soul, Motown, gospel, and so forth—was what everybody listened to. But the music played at the Rice mixers usually was the white rock music of the day, which wasn't the kind of music I liked or was used to. At first, it sounded like a lot of noise to me, but once I sat down and really listened to the great musicians the white students were playing on their stereos, I came to appreciate their talents and skills. After listening to Indian music for a while, for example, you can get into the groove and hear all the sounds the musicians have going on in the background.

By opening myself to music that was, at first, strange, I came to understand and appreciate it better, and that idea extends beyond elements like music to take in situations and people—whether alone or in groups. The point is, you have to give people and things a shot—even if they're foreign to you—before you race to judgment. If you do, you're more likely to discover new things that positively affect you and that lend you positive benefits.

Despite those mixers, I remained introverted. Maybe that goes back to those early years spent by myself at my grandmother's, but it also seemed like everybody was watching the black students and we were watching them, which kind of shone a spotlight on my introversion.

Everywhere we went and everything we did, people would be looking at us. That was something we just had to deal with. To be fair, though, it wasn't as if I went to these parties with a big smile on my face and offering my hand to everyone.

On top of all that, there were interactions between the few black kids there. Like I said, there were twelve of us—three of us football players—and I was pretty much the low man on the totem pole. I was okay with that because all this was strange to me, and I was trying to learn and ensure I passed my classes so I could make the football team. There was academic pressure, social pressure, economic pressure—just a lot of different stuff all at once—and it was all I could do to absorb everything and see who was who and what was what.

In general, my socialization went more smoothly than I'd anticipated. A few of my white friends did favors for me and even loaned me their cars on occasion—one a brand-new car with less than two hundred miles on it. I had many such interactions that amazed and touched me and just blew my mind about white people because where I'd come from, bad things can happen to you around whites. They didn't loan you their cars. They burned you up, blew you up, or hung you. So it was a new awakening to meet young white people and, for the most part, be treated like just another student. That amazed me.

Activities on the football field were another sort of learning experience. I was knocking down white guys who'd never been knocked on their butts by a black guy, and they were knocking me on my butt when I'd never had a white guy do that. But knocking each other down is what football players do, and everyone was respectful when they did it. It was definitely a lesson in real life—not just talking about equality but experiencing it at a basic physical level. That was the good side, and it occurred in an excellent academic environment and culture where, overall, people were respectful toward each other, even if we came from very different backgrounds. That was important for me because I had all these myriad and unfamiliar situations coming up, and I had to react to it all without any experience or training. I'd be lying if I said those days didn't test me and my understanding of who and where I was and what I wanted.

What I wanted was to play football. At that time, freshman players only played freshman football, not with the varsity. We had to prove ourselves both in training and academically. And of course, we went through all that freshman stuff, including hazing. Amusingly, all the hazing the varsity tried on us backfired. They came over to swap licks with a broom, for example, and I was paired off with this linebacker. When he swatted me, he didn't hit with flat of the broom but with its edge. That hurt a little, but my swat with the flat side lifted him off the ground. Undoubtedly, the freshman players got the best end of the hazing that year.

Even though things went fairly smoothly most of the time, I did have one confrontation with another player. We were all in the locker room one morning, drinking hot chocolate. This guy's cup got knocked over, and he wasn't happy about it because of his position—first team running back, if I remember correctly. He started making a lot of noise to me over the spilled chocolate, and I realized, *Here it is, the first confrontation—black, white, and all that stuff.*

I told him, "I didn't knock over your chocolate. Mike Tyler did that, so why are you acting so hostile?"

When I said that, all the other white players went, "Ooooh."

The guy confronting me said, "Pick it up," and I stood up and said, "Make me pick it up." I wasn't inclined to fight, but I guess everybody saw that I would and could if I had to. So we had this little standoff, but neither of us really wanted to fight, and it ended peacefully enough.

All this sounds straightforward, and maybe the situation wasn't all that unusual, but it did have racial components. The more obvious layer was that here was this young white man ordering a young black man to serve him and do his dirty work. In this regard, it didn't matter who'd knocked over the hot chocolate. I was there and was black, and the white player thought it was okay to order a black person to obey him. That was his error, but I didn't realize that I'd made my own cultural mistake—and maybe nobody else did either, at least in those terms, but it was there.

The thing is, in black culture, we were so obliging to authority that young people tended to tell the truth about their actions. That undoubtedly goes back to slavery, when lying to your owner could bring down corporal punishment or death. In black culture, if an adult asked you who did thus and such, you'd better tell them who did or face punishment of your own. So I was doing just that when I pointed out that it was Mike, not me, who'd spilled the cocoa. But in white culture, that was seen as an attempt to shift blame to someone else—ratting someone out—which isn't cool. That's the reason the white players all went, "Oooh!"

And there is yet another layer to this cake. When I said, "I didn't knock over your chocolate. Mike Tyler did that," what I actually heard coming out of my mouth was, "Yes, boss man. So-and-so did it." It immediately struck me that I'd sounded like an Uncle Tom snitching on someone. I knew that what I'd said was really messed up and gave the wrong message to everybody in the room. So I had to say, "Make me pick it up," to assert myself. If I hadn't issued the challenge, it would have looked like all the other parts were true, and those old attitudes and beliefs were what I was trying to get away from.

It took some time for me to understand those other layers, and the situation was a good example of how whites and blacks both had to come to grips with cultural differences. Thankfully, that was the only confrontation I had with my teammates. That running back ended up quitting the team, and if any of the other guys had a problem, they didn't call names or anything like that. And on the football field, I made it a point to demonstrate my skills so my coaches and teammates got a chance to see those and respect me for what I could do, so it was all cool.

As freshman players, we were mostly just biding our time with each other. The coaches started me as linebacker and offensive guard. I think I was third or fourth team. We had some really excellent freshman football players that year. There was Stahlé Vincent from Greensboro, North Carolina. The coaches brought him in to be the great starting quarterback for the Owls, and they put a lot of stock in him. He didn't pan out as a quarterback, though he ended up an All-SWC running back. Steve Woods was another good quarterback, and his abilities were pretty much on par with Stahlé's. Stahlé might have been a little bit better runner, but Steve had just as good an arm.

Mike Tyler moved up from the worst running back to the best, but after the first three plays of the first game, the coaches sat him on the bench, and that was pretty much it for Mike as a running back. They never let him start again, and they switched him to defensive back, so Mike got the short end of the stick even though he'd earned his way up.

It was odd how they did that to him because it was obvious they didn't want him as a starting running back even though he'd earned it. I think that shifting his position was the plan all the time. It was one of my first lessons in the way coaches can treat—or mistreat—their players.

The freshman players all started at the bottom of the chart and worked out together. There were around thirty-four of us. Colleges and universities could recruit as many players as they wanted, and some of the big schools recruited as many as a hundred freshman players a year because they didn't want other schools to snatch up any potentially good prospects. Then over the next few seasons, they'd weed out the weaker players. The thing was, though, once you got that athletic scholarship, it was yours as long as you maintained your academic record.

The freshman squad had only about six games on the schedule. The rest of the time, we were running dummy offense or defense plays with the varsity. Mostly what we did was running and conditioning, and it was competitive because everybody wanted to qualify for the starting team next year and make something of themselves. We'd begin each day early with a run, then we'd come in and take a short nap. After that, we'd get back to it late in the morning and work out for an hour or two, then take a break and come back that evening for more workout. So we started out with three-a-days, which means three practices a day, instead of the usual two. In between, we'd watch football films. That's what we did to get prepared.

The first game I played was against SMU in Rice Stadium. I didn't start, but they did put me in, and I played a little and had a good game. I went out for two or three passes and made a few hits and stops, so all of a sudden, I was in my coaches' good graces—even Coach Mayo was forced to recognize my abilities. It was funny observing the change in his attitude toward me after that first game. All of a sudden, we were tight, though that eventually faded away.

The rest of the season went okay, though it had its ups and downs. I wanted a linebacker position or maybe running back or strong safety—all positions that could take advantage of my speed, quickness, and other skills. I worked hard for linebacker, but they kept switching me back and forth between that and first-team offensive guard because we already had several outstanding linebackers. Those guys could really play. But if I wasn't going to get mine out of this deal, what the heck was I there for? Plus, I didn't want to play offensive guard. First of all, I wasn't tall or heavy enough, so for me to play that position was a waste of the coaches' and my time. In addition, had I tried for the pros in that position and actually made it, I would have been relegated to second or third teams. When you're that low on the roster, the coaches don't pay much attention to you beyond being their cannon fodder.

Besides, I knew that my talents and skills were more in tune with positions—like linebacker—that could take advantage of my speed and quickness. I could play linebacker in the pros. So the question was, how could I get out of being an offensive guard and maneuver myself toward the position I really wanted when we already had several good linebackers? In the end, I adopted a simple strategy: when they made me play offensive guard, I did a lousy job, and when I played linebacker, I played my best and made big plays.

Scholastic Realities

My socialization was going well, and my time on the football field was proving productive, but academics was where the problems came in. Rice has a reputation for high academic achievement, and after I was accepted by the university, I'd had a lot of anxiety about keeping up academically. When I got there, however, I learned that my education in many areas was up to par even though I'd been told all my life that black people were inferior. My ability to communicate with people helped, and I was intelligent, so I thought that succeeding academically would be just a matter of having the right attitude, learning, paying attention, and not stirring up the bus too much.

But the truth was, I was barely scraping by. That first semester, I made one B, two Cs and one D, and to keep my grade point average from going down even more, I ended up dropping another class that I was flunking. Of the thirty-four freshman football players that first semester, seventeen went on academic probation. They just couldn't hang with the strain and the stress. The university sent me a notice too, but they were in error since I'd dropped that one class. It seemed like they were already jumping the gun on trying to get rid of me too.

I resolved that issue, and thankfully, I learned how to study, so I was able to save my scholarship that first year. It was hard. I did well enough in the social sciences, but my literary skills remained weak, and I didn't have anyone to help me or correct my deficiencies in this knowledge-based area of study. So in some areas, I struggled, but in others, I could keep up and study enough to ask questions and so forth. Studying is tough when you're an athlete since so much of your time is taken up with practice and working out that it's hard to find adequate time for schoolwork.

Luckily, the athletic department paid some students to attend our classes and take what were called "jock notes" that were then shared with the athletes. Sometimes the notes were good, but sometimes they were just thrown together. It all depended on the pride of workmanship possessed by the kids who took the notes. But overall, the notes were helpful in condensing the most important facts and points. I just did my best.

Part of my problems with academics was the faculty. White students either had already made up their minds about the black students or tended to be inquisitive and wanted to know more about us. But students had no real power over you, so what they thought or said was relatively innocuous compared to how faculty or staff could treat you. To make matters worse, while a lot of the professors didn't like blacks, many also didn't like athletes, so I took flak from both groups. In addition, a lot of professors—particularly tenured professors— can be set in their ways. Too often they had traditional ideas about who black students were and what we might bring to the table. Some wouldn't talk to us anyway if we weren't one of their class favorites who hung around them. You could visit their offices and ask questions and get some direction every once in a while, but for the most part, they didn't know you or anything about you since they had grad students to handle a lot of personal interactions for them. You had to learn just by doing, so it was a struggle.

I had this one professor for American literature who was particularly open in his negative behavior toward me. As I've mentioned, literature was one of my academic weaknesses, and I struggled in his class. When he returned our work after we took a test or turned in a paper, he'd hold my test or paper high, bleeding all over with red marks, so that everybody could see the D or F at the top before he'd hand it to me. Even worse, he made absolutely no effort to help me correct my errors. So there I was, making the same F all semester long because he'd never explain anything to me.

In class, we'd read poems and stories by American writers who were very prejudiced toward blacks in their depictions. The professor read these passages aloud in a comical but stereotyped way and told jokes that made fun of African Americans, which he appeared to enjoy doing very much. The other students would turn red trying not to laugh at his supposedly comical portrayal of African Americans—of me. That was my first experience with a professor who was blatantly racist and did his best to humiliate me at every turn, including publicly exposing my bad grades, when he should have been helping and guiding all of us in our studies. That went on in literature for both of my freshman semesters.

The physical education department was just as bad. My major at the time was PE, and apparently, the department had never had an African American major—nor did they want one. One of my PE teachers definitely was not ready to accept integration. He acted as if, in me, the department had given him the worst of the worst. I had to take a class from him, so I knew that if I was going to pass PE, I'd really have to be on point all the time because this guy wasn't going to let a young black man come in there and be successful. Unfortunately, many of the PE faculty took the same attitude. They seemed to think that having an African American major weakened their department, and they did everything they could to prove that African Americans were physically, mentally, and academically inferior. When an African American matched or excelled over white students, they didn't know how to deal with that.

I guess I experienced resistance from some faculty members because they were free to do it. The faculty of a university should be there to share knowledge and to lead and guide students, but some of my professors seemed to be trying to fulfill and foster some kind of social conditioning by attempting to wedge African Americans into a preexisting but ill-fitting mold.

Maybe they were trying to prove something. You have to remember that back then, the answer to the question was, yes, the black man is inferior and incapable of achievement. Maybe they were trying to demonstrate that that answer was accurate and not just an opinion or some false social construct. In essence, they were trying to manipulate society in order to maintain white socioeconomic dominance over other racial groups.

Every once in a while, I had a professor who was straight up and cool, and that was refreshing, but too frequently, I found myself facing a wall of resistance. I hadn't anticipated the sort of reaction I was seeing. I guess I expected things to be done right and without a lot of politics, but I was naive. When these things started happening, I didn't fully understand the injustices, craziness, and all the rest that was going on, but I knew the situation wasn't right. And that started me thinking, *Wow, is there anything I can do to help myself?* Was there anyone at Rice who could help me and the other students like me who were struggling not just with academics but with cultural assimilation?

But there was no one. Despite the fact that this was a time of tremendous change for African Americans, the university didn't offer black students any assistance in acculturating to the environment. Today, Rice offers a tremendous amount of support to all its students, but this was not the case while I was there. There were no social services, no social groups, no outreach groups to help black students make the transition from their cultural backgrounds. It wasn't so much that Rice's administration didn't care about student support, but more that the need for it was something the university hadn't even considered, much less thought out. And blacks weren't the only ones left hanging. There also were Hispanics, Asian Americans, and international students, all of whom suffered a great deal too.

Truthfully, though, Rice didn't provide much at all in the way of services to any student, white as well as minority, but it was minorities and international students who suffered the most from the lack of a support infrastructure. Rice had been established to educate Caucasian Houstonians, and the culture of the university had emerged from the prevailing white culture, so white students already had a hand up over minority and international students in learning the Rice ropes.

Plus, Southern white culture encouraged the separation of the races, and consequently, there was little socialization between racial groups. This often left minority students at a loss when dealing with whites. In a culture that constantly belittles you, if you lack self-confidence and have difficulty talking to other people, then it can seem as if nobody wants to talk to you or acknowledge you because of racial differences. It's difficult to maintain a sense of self-worth in the face of constant degrading of one's character, personality, and abilities. To make matters worse, most of Rice's minority and international students didn't have the local personal connections and contacts possessed by many of the white students.

So I found myself at a university with almost no support for students. There was no instruction manual, nobody to go to, and nowhere to get help. Just as bad, some of the faculty really did not want African American students to succeed—even openly acting on that desire—which made it doubly hard to communicate with them. And with the promise of more and more minority and international students on campus over the next few years, the lack of a support infrastructure would become a significant problem for a growing number of students.

Then something happened that later gave me a whole new perspective on the matter as well as a way to correct it. Late in the summer of 1968, just before I started at Rice, the university's president, Kenneth Pitzer, stepped down to assume the presidency of Stanford University. It wasn't until February 1969, however, that the Rice Board of Governors named a successor—William H. Masterson. The board's decision proved unfortunate because few people at Rice wanted Masterson to be president. Some thought he was intellectually and personally unsuited to lead the university, and many faculty members and students also felt slighted in not having had a say in the decision.

Almost instantly, a huge, several-day protest rang out across the campus, accompanied by marches and speeches. The 1960s was an era famous for demonstrations on almost every front, with protest marches against segregation and the war in Vietnam and for women's liberation and equal justice. All that had largely escaped my attention, but now, I found myself being pulled into the Rice protest even though I didn't know anything about Masterson or the situation. People said that Masterson was no good, but I didn't really know why except that he'd given one of my suitemates an F+++ on one of his assignments. But there I was, out there marching with everybody else. It was my first involvement in trying to achieve social or political change on that scale. It was amazing to see students, faculty, and the rest of the Rice community involved and to witness the collective power they could bring to bear on the matter.

Within days, Masterson was forced to resign, and noted chemist Norman Hackerman was hired by popular consent early in 1970. Before coming to Rice, Hackerman had been president of the University of Texas, and after he left Rice in 1985, he served on the boards of several scientific organizations, including the National Science Board.

The whole Masterson Crisis, as it came to be called, was politics. In some ways, Masterson wasn't considered suitable, not because he was a bad guy, but because he wasn't approved of by those he would nominally lead. In a sense, it was democracy in action, and even though I didn't know anything about Masterson, the fallout from his appointment taught me the power of demonstration. It was my first lesson in getting personally involved in making changes on a large scale. I learned that right there at Rice, almost like an extracurricular course in art of social change, but at the time, I had no idea it would become a tool I'd eventually wield on my own crusade.

Sophomore Year

That crusade was still in the future when I arrived back at Rice in fall 1969 for my sophomore year. If I'd thought my first year was rough, the second hammered home the fact that I still had a whole lot to learn, including how to better regulate my own behavior. Returning to campus with a one-year-old Buick Riviera my mom gave me didn't help, and what little common sense I still possessed became masked beneath the great season I had in football.

In the beginning, I competed for a defensive right end position. The guy in front of me had made Second-Team All-SWC the year before, so he was a good player, which diminished my chances. But then, Coach Hagan brought in a couple of new coaches. My defensive end coach the year before had been Allen "Red" Bale, but the university moved him to assistant athletic director. The new defensive end coach, Gary Kinchen, decided to leap-frog me ahead of the guy who'd been starting. Defensive end wasn't the position I wanted, but I relished the chance to start. There was no way Red Ball would have done that, but Kinchen was new and interested in winning, so he put together a strong defensive line.

Our opening game, against Virginia Military Institute, was my first time to start for Rice. I ran about three plays, but I was hyperventilating due to my old heart condition, and I couldn't play any more. I just ran out of steam. So that first game was terrible, and by the end of it, I thought I'd lost my job on the team. But Coach Kinchen kept his faith in me.

The second game, we played LSU at Rice. I think they beat us 42–0, but I was back in form with something like twelve tackles and several other plays. I was running all over the place. Bert Jones was the quarterback for LSU, and he was a really great one, but when he tried to run my way, I was able to stop him. So even though we were beat badly, I had a pretty good game.

We went on and played top-ranked University of Texas at Austin, and I was put in as middle linebacker. The Longhorns were famous for running the Wishbone Formation, which, at the time, was considered the most effective offensive formation in college football. In fact, by 1970, UT had won thirty games and two national championships thanks to the Wishbone. But they didn't anticipate that the Owls would change up the defense and make them come out of the Wishbone, which was something that no other team had been able to do. I also like to think that my speed, quickness, and courage might have thrown off their game a little. We held them to no touchdowns until the fourth quarter, when they ran us out of the stadium. But even though we were defeated, I ended up having a decent game and was named Honorable Mention UPI Player of the Week.

My game against the Longhorns was the talk of the conference, and as the season progressed, my play was growing better and smoother. The coaches kept moving me back and forth between defensive end and linebacker, and what really helped me in that latter position was the great defensive line we had that year. But while we had a dynamite defense, our offense wasn't so hot. If they had been, we'd have won a lot more games. We went on to play Texas Tech, Arkansas, A&M, TCU, Baylor, and the others in the conference, and while we ended up winning only three or four times, I had great games. To my joy, not only was I named SWC Sophomore Defensive Player of the Year, but I also earned All-SWC Defensive Player of the Year as defensive end. I was the first African American defensive player to earn that award. Jerry LeVias, with Southern Methodist University, was the first to do it on the offensive side.

Coach Kinchen was at Rice for only one year, but he gave me the opportunity to start, to truly establish myself on the field, and to shine. Throughout the season, I was playing top-notch ball, and I thought I was popping. We might not have been winning overall, but I ended up playing the whole season, having a great time and a good year. My name was in the papers, and people were beginning to recognize my skills and abilities, but without Gary Kinchen's presence that one year, nobody would ever have heard of Rodrigo Barnes.

Despite all that, some elements within the university seemed not to want to acknowledge either me or my successes. All my negative feelings were compounded when the university's end-of-the-year awards were announced. I thought my great season and two SWC awards had proved I was worthy of the school awards. No other sophomore on the team had earned any major awards, and at best, they'd made All-Southwest Conference. But if the coaches are out there to make someone a star, and you outshine their boy, well, they don't know how to handle that. They might acknowledge that you had a great game, but they're not pulling for you, and they don't want to give you any award you might have earned. At least they didn't want to give one to me.

It's understandable, then, that I was a little frustrated with our coaches and sports information director when, despite my SWC awards, the university named another player, who hadn't earned any major awards, as Rice's sophomore player of the year. That really threw me off because I didn't understand that at all. I figured it wasn't a racial thing, though, because the guy who ended up with the award was another black kid. Just as bad, another player who'd only played a couple of games was named MVP, and I thought I should have gotten that too.

I realized that the university granted those awards for the public, not in the name of true achievement, but to me, it made the athletic department look foolish. Everybody had seen me play and win the SWC awards, and they had to wonder why the school publicly placed lesser players above me. Maybe part of that was because I didn't play spring football that year. Instead, I went out for track and threw the shot put and discus. I just needed to get away from football for a while, but back then you simply didn't do that. A lot of people were upset with me over that, which might have contributed to me being passed over for the school awards at the end of the spring semester. Whatever the reason, I have to think that giving awards to favorites instead of to people who have earned them degrades the whole purpose of awards.

By now, I was thinking, *Wow, what else is there in the world that I don't know about?* It seemed to me that the coaches were seeing what they wanted to happen instead of what was really happening. So they put me down on the sly because I was not what they wanted me to be. There I was, with major awards in the conference, and I came back to my home school, and the coaches were effectively telling me, "No, you weren't one of the best players on the team." For some reason, they just didn't seem to want to recognize me, and I didn't know what to think about that since socioeconomic and racial factors didn't appear to be involved. I couldn't wrap my head around it except to think that there was something within the school system that was anti–Rodrigo Barnes. It appeared that the very people who I thought were there to support and look after me were actually going against me in situations that should have been fair.

That was the kind of stuff I had to deal with. It was sad that I was making a name for myself on the field but that the people at my school—the very people I was winning for—didn't want to promote me or acknowledge my achievements. The whole thing really confused me, and I never fully got past it. Situations like that alter your way of thinking and erode your trust for other people. It also made me even less inclined to listen to advice when it was given, which intensified my hard-headedness. I thought I was protecting myself, but of course, not only was I ignoring advice, but I was also shutting out possibilities. And all that led to me to make bad decisions. That's what happened to me: I lost my trust of people, hampering my own development.

However, my social standing—off campus as well as on—had really grown, so I accepted the reality of the situation and thought everything was cool. Not only was I developing into a young man feeling his wild oats, but I also had a car, money in my pocket, and a bit of a reputation as one of the rising black stars at Rice University. I used to go down to Market Square, where all the gangsters and hippies hung out. I didn't know a lot about what was going on around me, and I guess a lot of people might have wondered if I was there to start something or just to have a good time. It was the good times I was after, and I wasn't messing with people or anybody's woman, though I didn't mind a little dancing.

Or I might be at the black clubs on Dowling Street at three or four in the morning, wondering why I was down there when I was supposed to be in class in a few hours. My answer was simple: I'm from the streets, and I'm comfortable there. It wasn't so much a matter of what I was doing; it's more a matter of observing and participating in what was going on around me. There might not always be a whole lot happening, but there was always something. My thing was to experience the reality of life. Did you see that? Did you hear that?

I guess I went crazy. I was going out all the time with a couple of classy, beautiful women, and other women were hitting on me everywhere I went. I hung out with sports figures and enjoyed the social life in Houston—mostly on the black side. As I loosened up, my philosophy changed enough for me to experiment with life, and in the process, I gained a whole new street education—and pretty much everything else—that year. I also discovered that a lot of people out there were jealous about the lifestyle I was living. That kind of surprised me, but I wasn't deterred.

I thought I was out there and doing it, but in the end, I went too far out and overdid it in many ways. I was messing around on the streets, enjoying life, having a good time, and kidding myself that I could do that and be a student at the same time. I knew I should have put a limit on my behavior, but I didn't. I missed a lot of classes that semester, and I ended up making three Ds and an F. My GPA hadn't been that hot to begin with, I was barely skating by, and the bad grades did me in. I'd let my pride, anger, and ignorance get the better of me and messed up everything. The result was probation. I was knocked off the team and off my scholarship, and I had to sit out football during the fall semester while I proved myself academically.

On the Probation Bench

I was devastated. I'd taken four courses—three in PE and one in biology—and I'd expected Cs, with maybe one D, instead of Ds and Fs. So there I went, off into a whole new bag of craziness—feeling sorry for myself and finger pointing—because I wasn't communicating with people. I'm judging as well as being judged and standing totally on the wrong footing.

A little reflection helped erase some of my naivete. I knew I'd ignored my better instincts, and that had been the beginning of my downfall. I was not prepared for success, and I was a little ticked off over the awards snub, and I let it affect me way more than I should have. I'd expected the granting of awards to be fair, but after all, those were their awards to give, not mine, and they could give them to anybody they wanted. It's not always about fairness or rightness but about who the coaches want to promote, and I wasn't that guy. Because there was no one around to explain things to me, I wasn't ready for any of this, and what I was looking for was something that doesn't exist. There I was, a black man in America, and I expected *what*? Man, I was lucky just to get recognized.

But the bad grades were largely my fault even though I believed that I hadn't always been treated fairly and was tempted to point fingers at this professor or that administrator. I shouldn't have let it happen, and I'd let myself down. I knew the rules and how things went, and I should have known better and done my work and stayed focused. A person has to make sure he or she is secure, and I didn't do that.

The point is that each of us has to take care of business if we expect to succeed and advance, and a large part of that is taking personal responsibility for our own actions instead of rushing to blame someone else. We cannot have excuses. Sure, there are many factors—racial, economic, social, and so forth—that we have to deal with, but if we're aware of those factors, we shouldn't have any excuses for not taking them into account. I knew the facts and situation, so what the heck was I crying about? In the end, all I could do was shoulder the responsibility.

No matter how I rationalized my situation, I still had to go somewhere for the summer, which meant Waco. My probation embarrassed my mom and friends, and there were a lot of "I told you sos" when I got home. I'd never experienced anything like that before. I definitely learned a lot about pride and humility that summer, and the experience forced me to assess where I was and what I wanted. I even considered transferring to another university—maybe the University of Southern California. In fact, I went to Baylor University that summer to make up my biology course.

But Baylor or some other school wasn't what I wanted. I wanted to continue at Rice. Rice is like that: once you're affiliated with it, it kind of sticks with you. When I returned in the fall, I'd have to drastically raise my grade point average to get back on scholarship and back on the team. It would take focus, dedication, and hard work, but I vowed to apply myself and not lose sight of the goal again.

My academic probation wasn't my car's fault, but I didn't like having the temptation of an easy out to get away from my real work, which was to regain my academic standing and scholarship and to achieve my goal of having a career in pro football. I gave the car back to Mom. During the summer, I worked at General Tire and Rubber Company to save money, putting in all the overtime I could. I didn't have a girlfriend or any other distractions, but Scotty Reese, my best friend from high school, was home for the summer from Marshall University. He also worked at General Tire, and we got to hang out a little. I just focused on trying to get enough money to get back into school because I felt I'd let down my mom and friends—not to mention myself—by flunking out.

Junior Achiever

By the time I went back to school, I'd managed to get a student loan, and I returned fully intending to succeed. I made some changes to help me keep on track, such as staying mostly on campus instead of going out. I had a few friends, and there were still a lot of things I could do if I wanted to, but I preferred to hang out at Rice and mingle with my fellow students, enjoying college life. I also had a little job on the side to help defray costs.

I took nineteen hours, which is a stiff load at any university, much less Rice. I did that because I wanted to bring my GPA back up and regain my scholarship. Since I was off the team, I didn't have football practice, which allowed me to concentrate more on school. I took a lot of 300- and 400-level courses, and I added sociology and behavioral science to my major in health and PE, so I was triple majoring.

Most days, I got out of class early in the afternoon and would go straight to the library for a couple of hours of study. After that, I'd go to the Rice Memorial Center, which was the building where students congregate, and hang out until dinner time. There I met a lot of different people—chicks, included— and found many friendships with other students. Some of these friendships were deeper than I'd experienced before, mainly because my earlier friendships at Rice had been with athletes and students who love athletes. When you're an athlete, you're sort of boxed in by scheduling, practice, meetings, and so forth, in addition to classwork, so you miss a lot and don't really get to experience college life to the fullest.

But that semester, I got a chance to do just that since I wasn't playing football. I hung out with the academs—as the liberal arts and social science students at Rice are called—and students interested in professional careers, and this gave me fresh new outlooks on life. It was a cool and beneficial semester for me, and I enjoyed being just a regular student. Another football player—a white guy by the name of Brownie Willis, who was an All-SWC tackle—and I even got involved in a play on campus. We only had small parts, but we enjoyed it, and I liked associating with the other actors. Later, my roommate, Mike Tyler, and I had the opportunity to participate in the filming of a couple of TV pilots. Those didn't go anywhere, but through them we got a little exposure to things other than football, and it was fun participating.

But also that fall, two tragedies occurred that made me think more deeply on life and how things can play out. On October 2, 1970, a plane carrying the Wichita football team crashed, killing everyone aboard. I'd almost gone to Wichita State, and if I had, I'd have been on that plane. I was in my dorm room when I saw the news, and suddenly it came to me that God had intervened and helped me miraculously raise my SAT scores because my being accepted to Rice literally saved my life. So out of that tragedy came a belief that I'd been saved for a reason and that my life had purpose. Something good was going to happen because I'd been saved.

But tragedy wasn't through with me. Less than six weeks later, on November 14, a plane carrying the Marshall University team crashed into a mountainside. That crash affected me just as much because my best friend, Scotty Reese, was on that plane. I felt especially bad since I hadn't talked to him in a couple of months. When those two crashes happened, they made me stop and reflect on might-have-beens and roads not taken. In looking at some events in your life, you have to give thanks because the situation could have turned out very differently.

By the end of the semester, the lowest grade I made was one C. The rest were As and Bs, so I immediately went back on scholarship and back on the team. But that one semester of just being a regular student at a great university with great things going on was really wonderful. I wish I could have spent more time like that after football season, but that's not the way it works when coaches are involved. They have to win, and you're there to help them do that and put on a show. That's what it's all about, and I was ready to do my part.

That was easier said than done. I'd been out a whole season, so I needed to work hard to get back in top form. To skew matters more, that January, Rice hired a new head coach: Bill Peterson. Peterson replaced nearly the entire coaching staff with guys he brought from Florida State. My new linebacker coach was Bobby Ross. He'd coached for a several universities before he came to Rice, and later he coached in the pros for a number of years. Al Conover, was the new offensive line coach. Only Jake Hess, the coach who'd recruited me from Waco, remained from the former staff.

The team returned to Rice in August to prepare for the regular season. When I actually started playing again in the 1971 fall season, my football eligibility was out of sync with my academics due to the events of the past year. Academically, I was officially nearly a senior, but I was just beginning my second real year of football since freshman students don't get to play varsity.

It was a demanding season. In addition to concentrating on academics and taking all these advance courses, I was doing a lot of hard work in practice to show the new coaching staff that I could play. Once I did that, I had a great year, and they began to respect and like me. And so did the fans. The student newspaper, the *Rice Thresher*, had this to say in late September: "Rice's defense, led (of course) by

Rodrigo Barnes, Dale Grounds, Randy Alford, and Bruce Henley, performed marvelously all through the game." And a quote in *Sallyport*, the university magazine, from that same season read: "The new 4-4-3 alignment has been spearheaded by the return of Rodrigo Barnes to middle-linebacker. The 6'2", 215-pounder has been an outstanding performer for the Owls, constantly leading the team in tackles and assists. Barnes is an excellent defender against both the short pass and the rush, and his blitzing tactics have, on several occasions, caused opponents to fumble. Rodrigo is a cinch all-SWC choice this year, and with some luck, could be a future All-American performer." I loved playing in Rice Stadium. It's a huge arena, at the time able to seat about seventy thousand. It's big enough that Super Bowl VIII was played there in 1974. It's also the place where President John F. Kennedy made his famous 1962 speech about the United States going to the moon. The Owls played all our SWC rivals there, and I especially liked playing the big games: LSU, Texas A&M, Texas Tech, Arkansas, and Texas. Games against SMU always filled the stands because of their strong playing in the late 1960s. Games against our local rivals, the University of Houston, always drew a nice crowd too. If we were playing a lesser team, we might only have twenty or twenty-five thousand spectators, but we sometimes topped fifty thousand when we played the more competitive teams. I got used to playing in front of big crowds in Rice Stadium, and I liked being in that arena.

By the end of the 1971 season, I'd been named SWC Player of the Year and All-SWC Linebacker. As far as I know, I'm the only person to make All-SWC in two positions: as defensive end for the 1969 season and as middle linebacker for 1971. I also received Rice's Jess Neely Defense Award, named for the coach who'd led the Owls from 1940 to 1966. Rice nearly went to a bowl game in 1971, but we didn't quite make it thanks to a tie with Arkansas in Rice Stadium. If we'd won that one, we'd have had a chance, but in the end, we won only six games, and you need seven to go to a bowl.

All in all, having had a rigorous off-season of academics and training then being challenged to prove myself to the new coaches turned out to be another excellent learning experience. But there was a lot I hadn't learned, and it seemed that none of my efforts to correct the issues in my life had done much to change my personality. The truth was, I was in awful mental shape. When you're competing in football, you have to stay focused and stay strong, and your mind is so far out there, it's unreal. And when you're twenty or twenty-one, you think you know, but you don't know, and you're sure to mess up. That's where I was by the time I was twenty-one: filled with pride and ego, unknowing, out there, and unable to see the truth about myself. That was the terrible part because when you don't see yourself, you can't change the things that you need to change. But that doesn't mean you can't see things that need changing in the outside world.

My entire first year of college had been extremely difficult. On top of tough academics, learning how to study, working hard on the football field, and dealing with social and cultural situations that were completely new to me, I hadn't had many people to socialize with. I didn't have a car or a TV or even a radio. There was no money, and when you're broke, you can't go anywhere. I didn't have anything or anyone. I was just trying to stay afloat in the currents of the many transitions and challenges that had caught me up, all while doing my best to pass my courses and play football. I didn't want to fail in the challenges I'd undertaken.

It was an intense period of learning and discovery, and one of the most important things I found out, as I've mentioned before, was that the university wasn't providing leadership in supporting students who were struggling with issues of race, culture, and socialization, not to mention academics. In fact, the first black undergraduate admitted to Rice, Gloria Oliver, ended up dropping out after only a short time because she had no support system. But while the administration appeared to be oblivious to the situation, affected students had to face tremendous issues. And I was one of them.

During my semester off from football, I spent a lot of time talking to other African American students, listening to their problems, and trying to do something to get them the help they needed. That went on for a year or so, and I was happy to help since the university didn't provide leadership in that regard. It seemed that I'd effectively become Rice's unofficial social worker, though I'm not sure I thought of it that way then.

By the time I was a junior, though, I found that everybody was leaning on me and wearing me out. I knew that my solo efforts weren't enough, and besides, I was only twenty-one, and what the heck did I know? Well, I did know one thing. I knew it would take a team effort, just as it took a team effort to win in football, just as it had taken a team effort to force the university to replace an unpopular Rice president. I realized my fellow students needed some sort of organization, and I began working toward that goal. If there were no student support groups on campus—either established by the university or by the students themselves—I would have to use what I'd learned about protest during the Masterson Crisis to establish one.

I might be generally somewhat introverted, but I've also always been outspoken, and now I had something to focus that on. I began speaking out to the university—students, faculty, and administration alike—on the deeper issues of race, which could be quite a bit more complex than simple black-and-white. Rice's black undergraduate student population had grown since I was a freshman as the university admitted more minorities and international students. Even so, while I was at Rice, the number of African American undergraduates never passed the midthirties—and that included athletes, who made up a third or more of the total black student population.

With that growth came diversity, even within supposedly homogenous groups. I met a lot of black kids who came from backgrounds, schools, cultures, and economic situations that were strange to me. In general, that wasn't a problem for me or anybody else. Nobody cared, and everybody did what they wanted to do. But sometimes, it resulted in black students who didn't want to associate with other black students but preferred to hang out with white kids.

This is perfectly illustrated by an attractive young black woman who'd just entered Rice. Most of the African American students tried to be friendly and establish contact with her, but she wasn't having any of that with me or the other African American boys who spoke to her. I'd say hello, and she'd completely ignore me and turn away. At first, I didn't get it, but over time, it seemed that she looked down on me. Maybe that was because she had a white boyfriend. Whatever the reason, her attitude bothered me since I'd never before experienced racial resentment from anybody in my own race.

That had an impact I never forgot. I didn't hold any animosity toward her; I just didn't understand. It bothered me also because, by this time, I'd been joined by other like-minded African American students in organizing Rice's black students into a group that would provide unity, assistance, and recognition for all of us. Some of those students were Jan West, Leroy Sterling, Frederick Foster, and Regina Tippens. It wasn't as if we were trying to force anyone to join or anything. That was up to the individual, though ironically, I was the only black athlete in the group. But we were fighting for all of us, and we needed all the internal cohesion and support we could get. Above all, we needed black administrators and faculty at the university who we could relate to and who could help us deal with the racial issues we faced, which were always present though not always obvious.

We did a one-day picket to appeal to the university to hire a black coach and African American administrators who could provide guidance as well as justice. I'd say that nearly three-fourths of the black students on campus were involved in the demonstration. Even though our numbers were relatively small, in the end, we were successful in getting a black basketball/football coach hired. It turned out that he did know something about basketball, but not much about football. The university also hired a professional staff person to help black students adjust to life in predominantly white Rice.

During this time, I had several personal discussions about these issues, not only with our athletic director but also with Rice president Norman Hackerman. He was an avid racquetball player, and I frequently ran across him in the gym, where we often spoke with each other. When I decided to be more proactive in getting involved in racial issues and letting Rice know that black students were here and needed support, I spoke to him about those matters.

Our discussions frequently centered on money—or the lack of it—for student support. I pointed out that the government granted the university funds to assist in taking care of the needs and social well-being of students though activities and such. But aside from sports, there weren't any activities on campus that appealed to me. The solution, I suggested, was to allow me and other like-minded students to use our share of the funds to start a support organization for black students that offered events and programs that did interest us. So Rice did that, and we had a few little affairs, such as Easter egg hunts and parties, not only to give ourselves a way to socialize but to give white kids at the university a chance to socialize with us. Those were successful and began opening the university to black culture.

The efforts I spearheaded finally morphed into the first official student support group on campus: the Black Student Union, today called the Black Student Association. I served as the organization's first president, and I had several reasons for helping lead the charge, not the least of which was that I was personally affected on multiple levels. But other elements came in, including my social standing on campus. Even though I tended to have a personality that turned inward, I quickly learned that as soon as I started speaking out, others came to me because they had to go to somebody, and I was about it as far as Rice went. I wasn't just an outstanding jock anymore—I was a cultural leader invoking change. That sounds nice, saying it from the safe distance of nearly fifty years, especially since Rice, which has come a long way from the inception of the BSU, honors me for it, now. These days, the university has numerous support groups, many of which fall under the Office of Multicultural Affairs, but back then, I had one tough row to hoe.

In the end, though, I found myself in a dilemma. My activism had helped found the BSU, but now too much was happening in my life for me to continue. I had my grades to maintain, and football occupied a great deal of my time since I still had my sights set on a berth with a pro team, so I had to step back from the BSU. Another student, Leroy Sterling, took the reins and did an excellent job after I went back to concentrating on football. He's now a cardiologist in the Texas Medical Center.

In the end, I'd have to say that my junior year was productive. I'd helped establish student life as an important element of Rice's structure, I'd done well academically, and I had a really great year in football. So I was feeling good about everything, not the least of which was my bouncing back from probation, when bam, the bottom dropped out of everything.

Played Out

It started when almost all our coaches—most of whom had only been with the Owls for a year—suddenly left. Bill Peterson jumped ship to the Houston Oilers, though he lasted only a little more than a year there. After that, his coaching career tanked, and he became an athletic director at the University of Central Florida. Most of the other coaches joined other pro teams too. My linebacker coach, Bobby Ross, went on to become the head coach for several college and pro teams such as the Kansas City Chiefs, San Diego Chargers, and Detroit Lions. That left us stuck with our former offensive line coach, Al Conover, as head coach. He was a young man who hadn't had much social interaction with people of other races, so he'd never really developed a way of understanding and working with African Americans. It's no surprise, then, that there was a lot of friction between him and some team members in that regard—especially wide receiver Ed Collins, who was drafted by the Indianapolis Colts in 1974.

But Conover was amusing, too, in an unintentional way and could get very energetic while trying to hype up the team. Once when we were about to play Arkansas, he got so worked up that he threw a chair through the window in the locker room. He wasn't always so physical, but maybe it worked that one time because we won the game. More usual was this ritual he put us through before every game. It was called "the tree." No matter where we were—playing at home or away—the evening before the game, he'd take us out into some nearby woods where he'd pick a tree. As we all stood around the tree, he'd give us a speech about it and how its parts—trunk, roots, branches, and leaves—all worked together to make a whole tree. It was his way of psyching us up to work together, but I thought it was pretty funny and had to look down most of the time to keep from losing it and getting in trouble for making fun of his pep talk.

Despite my amusement at that, all in all, my senior year in football was a miserable experience. As a player, I'd made a lot of friends and received a lot of support, but I also saw a lot of haters out there. When you're a college freshman or sophomore player, everybody loves you, but when you reach your junior and senior years, there are new freshman and sophomore players coming up through the ranks, and folks don't love you as much because they're too busy loving the new guys. So now I was discovering another learning experience as the coaches tried to move me out and move somebody else in.

I shouldn't have played that season anyway. I ended up hurting my right knee—cartilage damage—and came away from a game against LSU with a bruised kidney. The problem was that a lot of the other guys weren't really playing. Maybe they'd been demoralized by the sudden departure of the coaching staff. Whatever the reason, we were still out there on the football field, and everybody should have been doing their jobs to the best of their abilities. I was a very aggressive player, and if you're an aggressive linebacker, you're counting on your teammates to make a certain level of effort because, in many ways, you're playing off them. It's hard to make good plays when the guys who are supposed to be running interference on the front line aren't doing their jobs. That was the general state of things that year, and because the linemen didn't do what they were supposed to do, I got hurt back to back, taking me out near the end of the season.

It was time for an assessment. On the negative side, I had all these injuries, Conover and I weren't getting along, and he was bad-mouthing me and calling me a troublemaker. Plus, it had been just a crazy, terrible, and busy year. On the positive side were my determination and stubborn nature. I wasn't about to quit. The time for the pro draft was quickly approaching, so I stuck it out.

Another tough thing was that, because I'd lost academic time by failing those courses during the fall of my sophomore year, I was behind most of the guys I'd known through college. They were now gone, and that included Mike Tyler, who'd moved out of the dorm. But that vacancy in my life didn't last long. Before Mike moved out, another football player, Harry Higgins, approached me and said he understood that I would be without a roommate the next year. Would I mind if he moved in? I said, "Sure."

Harry was about 6' and 215 and had played football for Worthing High School in Houston. As a Rice running back, he was a hard worker, had heart, and wouldn't quit or give up. And he ran the ball pretty well. Best of all for me, he was a wonderful guy with a good heart. The more we got to know each other, the closer we got, and he turned out to be one of my strongest supporters and friends. He didn't make me out to be a hero; he just wanted to understand who I was and what I was about. In turn, I had great respect for Harry. We liked each other, and we shared a lot about ourselves. Plus, Harry loved to have a good time, and we often went places together and had fun.

You couldn't have a better friend, and that was something I really needed at the time. Harry's a hell of a man, and the only bad thing I can say is that he was my roommate for too short a time. That semester, he took a test to go into military service—I think it was for officer training school—and he ended up enlisting in the Marine Corps. Two weeks later, he was out of there. But we've kept in touch over the years, and he showed up for my Rice University Hall of Fame ceremony, still supporting me.

The Pro Draft

The day of the pro draft, I got up around nine o'clock. I was projected to go in the third round, but you really need the support of your coach to make the early rounds, and Conover certainly wasn't doing any cheerleading for me, to say the least. At the time, the Houston Oilers were members of the American Football Conference, and draft prospects could watch the draft live at their building, which was right next to the Oilers' practice facility. A lot of prospects went there, but I decided to stay in my dorm room. By now, I was the only one there since Harry had gone into the Marines, so I sat alone in my room to see what would happen.

I wasn't nervous, exactly, but I couldn't help but reflect on the situation I'd put myself in over the last year or two through picketing the university and all the other things that had gone down. I felt that I hadn't done well, and I realized that all that might have hampered my efforts to turn pro. It's often been speculated by others that my prospects were dimmed by my civil rights activism in college and my outspoken nature. I think there might have been some truth to that. Not only was Al Conover bad-mouthing me all over the NFL, but I also was slandered in a 1973 book about the 1971 Owls, *Saturday's Children*.

My teammate, Jerry Butler, was drafted by the Kansas City Chiefs in the second round as tight end, so that was one good piece of news. But the third round came and went without my name coming up, and so did the fourth, fifth, and sixth, and I began to get a little nervous. If you're not drafted by the end of the first day—by the end of the seventh round—that puts a lot of pressure on you and makes things difficult for your future in pro football.

Finally, just as the day was drawing to a close, the Dallas Cowboys called me to say they'd selected me in the seventh round. I was a little disappointed—and humbled—at being called so late, but I was relieved and excited, too, at the prospect of being a Cowboy under Coach Tom Landry.

The news couldn't have come at a better time. I loved Rice, but I'd been there too long and had become a problem. The administration was mad because I'd picketed the university and made them hire a black coach. I'd "persuaded" the administration to do something they didn't want to do, and they hadn't experienced much of that before—especially from African Americans. All I'd really done, though, was to practice what I'd learned about the power of demonstration from the university's own lesson plan: the Masterson crisis.

The crazy thing is that right was wrong then, though it's right now. If a white boy did something that pushed the envelope, he was a heck of a leader and a good boy, but when I did the same thing, I became an outcast. I have to admit, though, that I was kind of clueless about all this. All through high school and college, I just competed. I knew I was black, but I didn't care what color I was. I was just out there playing and doing what I do. But in the end, I paid a price both ways, often being the brunt of a wrong then being punished when I tried to rectify that wrong and do what I thought was right. Worse, too frequently the punishment had a strong element of hatred to it. It was crazy. Everything that I get awards for these days, the Rice administration was upset about back then.

Some of that certainly was my own fault. I admit I have a strong personality, and people can have a hard time dealing with me. I had to come to the realization that I couldn't be the way I was and think the way I did without offending people and bearing potentially dangerous consequences. That hurt. I was perceived as offensive and sometimes out of step because I didn't always go for what society said is good and right but insisted on seeing things by my own lights. As a consequence, brothers pretty much ran from me because they didn't want to get in trouble with the white man, and white people pretty much stepped back, leaving me sitting right there in the middle, just being my natural self.

Maybe I was that way because I'd never had a mentor and was used to figuring out things on my own. I did talk to my mom about different things, but there were so many elements in my life, so many opportunities going on, and so many things to do and do right that she had no experience with. I had only a few friends, and my relationships with girlfriends were mostly back and forth and not really genuine. Up to that time, I never had a girlfriend who'd been hundred-percent, and I was a 24-7-365 and hundred-percent type of guy. That's what I wanted and what I expected of a woman, and if I didn't have that, I found I just couldn't trust what was going on. I guess you could say that I'd never had a successful relationship. It also meant that I didn't have anyone to confide in except the man in the mirror.

I didn't think I'd have much success trying to change my personality, so I decided I'd simply have to go on being me and try not to mistreat, use, or take advantage of others. People would just have to deal with me as I was. It came as no surprise to me, then, that the athletic department was ready to see the end of me. It was "push me out" time from all sides.

Fortunately, by my second senior semester, I'd completed all the classes I needed to graduate, though I took one class anyway so I could keep a dorm room on campus. I finished my classwork in April, and after that, I was just doing time, waiting to go to the Cowboys. It was a strange interval. I'd done some things right. I'd made it to this point in life, and things were okay on the outside. I was finishing college and had an opportunity to play professional football, so I had a job. The big question hanging over me was what position would I get? Would it be middle linebacker, the only position I really wanted?

Rice's graduation ceremony usually is held outside in the university's main quadrangle, but when the day arrived, the skies opened up and poured down rain. The ceremony was held in the gym instead. Attending was nice for me because, even though I'd gone on probation, I'd come back and managed to graduate with a triple major under my belt. I was proud, my mom and sister were there, and my dad flew in from California. A few of my other relatives were there, too, so I had a small crowd to cheer my success when they announced my name. Even some of the faculty and administration had come to respect me to one degree or another, and some of them showed me love.

So it was a great moment. On the education side, I had BAs in sociology, behavioral science, and H&PE. On the social side, I'd help found the BSU. And on the sports side, I was named All-SWC Running Back of the Year in 1969 and All-SWC Linebacker of the Year in 1971. The former makes me the first African American to win a SWC Defensive Player of the Year Award, and the latter makes me the only person I know of to win the All-SWC Defensive Player of the year award in two positions. In addition, I was twice named All-SWC Defensive Player of the Year. I also was named SWC Second-Team All-Decade for the 1970s and Second-Team UPI All-American Linebacker. And finally, UPI had named me player of the week several times during my college career. With all that, I ought to be in the SWC Hall of Fame, but I'm not.

Rice, however, honored me for my athletics on October 21, 2011, when I was inducted into the Rice Athletic Hall of Fame. Later, on October 1, 2016, I was a guest of honor at Rice University's Blueprint for Excellence Gala, where I was presented with the Legacy Award for my outspoken efforts to improve the lives of black students—and by extension, all students—by helping establish the Black Student Union and for doing my best to encourage the university to hire black teachers and coaches. But that was in the future and inconceivable to me at the time. All I could concentrate on when I graduated was that I was going to the pros.

Graduation also was a very sad moment because I was leaving a wonderful institution with excellent academics, populated by many very fine people—both students and faculty—who were generally very nice, inoffensive, and supportive. On top of that, the university had learned to listen to some of its marginalized voices. The administration and the protesting students didn't always agree, and we didn't always give in or get our way, but the administration listened and replied.

And they did not destroy me. They could have destroyed me, and they did not. They said, "If you can make it academically and don't get in trouble, then you can stay." When I went on academic probation, I knew it was mostly my fault because I should have made sure I was doing the work, and I didn't. I should have made sure about the professors I was taking classes under and made sure of the possibilities, and I didn't. So I blame myself for that and nobody else. But I did return, and a lot of Rice folks welcomed me back.

The truth is that I couldn't have survived out in the world on my own back then—at least not the way I was. I needed a place of transition to learn who I was and how to regulate myself—a place as free from unnecessary impediments as possible. Going to Rice was a tremendous boost to my self-esteem because it made me somebody, even if it was only to myself. I couldn't have done that out in the real world, at least not right out of the gate. At Rice, I learned to work hard and be a part of something larger than myself. It was a period of tremendous development in my life, and I grew so much from my experiences there. I had a freedom in which I was treated like a citizen of the United States, not like an inconsequential black person. Students were respectful, and all around me were honest and fair minds. Even the administration had softened toward me. If they hadn't exactly liked what I'd done, they still saw me and my requests for change on campus as worthy of consideration.

I should have gotten more out of Rice than I did, and I wish I'd established more relationships there, but even so, it was just a wonderful experience, and I didn't want to leave. That's why I took that unnecessary last class—it allowed me to keep my dorm room for one final semester. But when graduation was over, I had to pack up and leave.

CHAPTER

7

THE BLUE–GRAY FOOTBALL CLASSIC

Before I left Rice, though, I had my introduction to pro sports. That was the now-defunct annual Blue–Gray Football Classic, a contest between all-stars from Northern and Southern colleges—the Blues and the Grays. Players from Western colleges usually played alongside the Blues. It was an introduction to pro sports because players were paid a little to participate, so it tended to draw only seniors who weren't worried about their college eligibility. The game, which was played sometime in late December, usually on Christmas day, had been conceived in 1939 by college football legend Champ Pickens, and it ran from then until the early 2000s, when it petered out due to lack of television sponsorship. Until the Blue–Gray Classic's last year, all the games were played in the Crampton Bowl in Montgomery, Alabama.

Being from a Southern college, I was on the Gray team, which was kind of ironic—and doubly so since we were playing in Montgomery, Alabama. Our coach, Billy Tohill, was just coming off his last year as head coach at TCU. The teams traveled to Montgomery nine days before the game, and during that time, the two teams stayed in different hotels. Actually, calling them hotels is generous. Motels was more like it. Ours wasn't all that nice, and it was out on the edge of town instead of being situated someplace where we could get out and meet people.

Nine days is a long time to prepare for a game. Usually you have only five or six days at the most. We worked out every day, and afterward, we'd go back to the motel. The first couple of nights, I noticed that somebody was coming to the motel, picking up the white players, one or two at a time, and taking them off somewhere. The black players, on the other hand, were stuck in the motel with nothing to do and nobody coming to visit us. There was no party. There was no nothing. For the black players, it was work hard all day then go back to the motel and hang out while the white players disappeared.

I asked a couple of our white teammates about what was going on. These guys happened to be from up North—maybe New York or Chicago—but they'd gone to Southern schools and so were on the Gray team. They didn't mind opening up a little bit, and they let me know what the deal was. While we black players were marooned in this motel out in the middle of nowhere, the white players were being shuttled off to big parties and galas out at the country club and other fancy places.

Up to this time, I'd been alone in my room since my roommate, Tommy Jackson, hadn't yet arrived. He was running a couple of days late due to a prior commitment. Tommy was from the University of Louisville, and he went on to play for the Denver Broncos. Later he was an award-winning ESPN sports commentator, for which he was inducted into the Pro Football Hall of Fame. By the time Tommy showed up, I was fuming. Around day three, I told him, "I'm getting ready to call Tohill and tell him I'm about to go home—and some of the other players too—because the way we're being treated is wrong. We're supposed to be among the best college players, and we're working hard and putting on a show just like everybody else, yet we're stuck out here in the boondocks with nothing to do. Most of us aren't from Alabama, and we're not used to this kind of treatment."

Coming from Houston and having liberated myself through my own efforts and the kindness of a lot of other people, I'd been privileged in a lot of ways. I was a star athlete from a top-notch college, and I'd grown tremendously since my days in the projects in Waco. And since then, I'd had real experience in fighting racial injustice. You know by now that I can be, let's say, feisty, and I'd grown comfortable enough with confronting people about situations of injustice to put myself out there and on the line.

But I was largely alone. At that time, most of the guys were concerned with being drafted and making it in pro football, so they were sucking up to everybody—coaches, managers, veteran players—and trying not to make waves. But I didn't look at football like that. Football was something that I liked to do, and I did it, but if I hadn't, I'd have done something else. Furthermore, if I did play football, I wasn't about to give up any part of my freedom or any of the privileges I held as an American citizen, period. I was adamant about that. It wasn't something that I went around preaching, but it was the personal code I'd come to live by. I knew that code would cause me troubles here and there, but I was willing to suffer the consequences, as I'd occasionally done at Rice and, in some ways, in high school. Maybe I was naive in thinking like that, but that's where my head was.

When you're an athlete, you tend to confront all difficulties with combativeness, but not all situations can be resolved like that. Some people are adamant in the opinions they hold, but the positions of many others can be shifted through reasoning, understanding, respect, and

appreciation. If you can just get them to listen, then you're more likely to achieve your goals than through combativeness. Martin Luther King Jr. and Mahatma Gandhi are examples of people who peacefully confronted authority and largely succeeded in their aims. But I didn't understand that kind of thinking yet, so I approached this situation combatively, and that was not smart.

I called Tohill and told him what was happening. I said, "We're not up here making a difference. You are. Montgomery, Alabama, is making the difference. The governor is making the difference. You are the ones dividing us and running the white kids to parties while us black kids are just sitting around doing nothing." I went on to say that the black players weren't going to be treated like this. If they didn't provide something for us do, I, at least, was going back home.

That evening, just a couple of hours after the phone call to Tohill, Tommy and I were lying around in our room, trying to figure out what we could possibly do since there was no one to do anything with, nowhere to go, and no transportation to get there, when a knock sounded on the door. Tommy opened it, and there stood a 5'10"—in heels, about 6'1"—blond, blue-eyed white girl in an outfit that looked like a Santa Claus helper's suit with a minidress. She was fine and pretty and had personality, and I think she was a former Miss Alabama. She was just a super young lady. I guess she was going to a Christmas party, which was why she was dressed like that.

"Is Rodrigo Barnes here?" she asked.

I perked up and said, "Yeah, that's me."

She walked in and came over to me and said, "I'm here, Rodrigo, to tell you we're going to have some celebrations for you guys. We'll start with a party tonight."

I looked at Tommy, and he looked at me, and I said, "Well, all right." Then I said to her, "Baby, I just want to know one thing."

She said, "What's that?"

And I said, "Are you here for me?"

She smiled and said, "No, I'm sorry. But I'll give you a little kiss." So she gave each of us a little kiss on the cheek and big hugs, so it was all good.

She left, and we all got ready to party. After a little while, this black chick named Sandi drove up in a GTO. She was my date. She was a pretty girl, a little older than me, with polish and experience. I think she'd done some modeling up in Boston. It seemed that she'd been at the party for the white players before she'd left to pick me up. I had the impression she was the kind of pretty black girl that rich white boys and players liked to have hanging around at parties.

I asked her if she wanted to go to the party that had been arranged for the black players, and she said she didn't. I think she'd had enough partying for one night. She suggested we hang out at her house instead. I ended up staying with her the rest of the time I was in Montgomery, so it was funny that I never did go to any of the parties I'd insisted on having for the black players. But after that year, the Blue–Gray Classic's organizers made sure that everybody on both teams was provided with equivalent amenities.

I was happy that I'd helped break another racial barrier, but at the same time, the incident damaged me because there I was again, out there negotiating for black people, and white folks just didn't like that. This is America, where many people said that if you're black, you are ignorant, can't do certain things, and can't put your own interests first. With that going on all the time, it's hard to fight the belief that those people are right. I thought I'd moved past all that because I insisted on being treated equally with whites and wanted an integrated environment where people showed respect for each other. That's what I'd come from at Rice. But really, I couldn't move past it—not until America improved its mindset.

But there wasn't any fallout from Tohill—at least none that was obvious. And despite my protest about the black players not being treated equally, Tohill named me as the Gray team's cocaptain. I don't know. Maybe he was impressed with my initiative. Anyway, we went on and played the game, and not only did we win, but I also was named defensive player of the game. Maybe more importantly, I met and played with some of the other rookies who'd been drafted by the Cowboys that year—guys I'd be playing alongside when the fall season began.

The following April, I got together with Gil Brandt to sign my contract. Brandt was the Cowboys' vice president of player personnel, which meant he was their chief talent scout, and he was the first guy I met with the Cowboy organization. He'd been with the Cowboys since the beginning and worked with them until 1988. In 2019, he was inducted into the Pro Football Hall of Fame. On the surface, Gil had a solid personality, but underneath was a hardness, particularly regarding money. Although he enjoyed being with the Cowboys, the things he had to deal with in his position didn't seem to make him very happy.

Gil's contribution to the Cowboys was to pay the players as little as possible. Back in those days, we had to sign three consecutive one-year contracts. It wasn't much of a deal for the players. I got a little signing bonus. I think it was $12,000, though taxes reduced that to something like $8,000. My first year's salary was $20,000, so you could say that I wasn't at all impressed with the pay. But even if I didn't like it, that was the deal the Cowboys offered, so I went ahead and signed. The salary went up about $4,000 a year for the second and third years, and I did have a few incentives, which are clauses in your contract that give you extra money for making good plays, such as recovering fumbles, making touchdowns, and so forth.

I thought that I really should have had more incentives than I did. On my first year with the Cowboys, I made two or three qualifying plays on both the defensive and special teams—as many plays as anybody else. A play is a play no matter where you do it, and while each one can add to your paycheck, each one also can get you hurt. At that time, though, I wasn't thinking about injuries, only playing. Ironically, thanks to that incentive money and my signing bonus, I was paid a lot more for my first year than for my second, even though my baseline paycheck went up the second year.

I gave some of my signing bonus to my mom and used some of the rest to rent a little one-bedroom apartment in the Village Apartments in north Dallas. It was the same complex where Billy Joe DuPree lived. I spent most of my last semester commuting back and forth, working out, and making plans, and when I graduated from Rice, I moved permanently to Dallas to take up residence. After the relative racial harmony of the university, I found myself thrown back into an environment where, all of a sudden, I was a nigger again.

Part Three
The Dallas Cowboys

Chapter

8

A Cowboy Summer

It was now the beginning of June, and from then until the first week of July, when we were scheduled to fly out to training camp, I lived in Dallas. Most of my time was spent hanging out with some of the other guys who'd been drafted that year and working out, trying to prepare myself for training camp so I could make the team. The first three draft rounds automatically made the team unless somebody got hurt, while the guys in the other rounds up to the seventh—myself included—might make the special teams if we worked hard and showed that we had the right stuff. Most of us in this precarious situation remained only prospects in the eyes of the coaches, and I was just one of the guys they took on, hoping that I might measure up.

The idea that I might not measure up never entered my equations, though, because I wasn't there just to be there. My stuff was good and I knew it, and the only question I had was whether or not the coaches were going to let me play to prove myself. My personal goals of playing starting middle linebacker, however, seemed distant because the Cowboys didn't appear to be looking for another linebacker—left, right, or middle. But I didn't let that put me off. I hadn't known anything else but starting and playing nearly my entire college career, and I was set on the same thing in the pros. Sitting on the bench was foreign territory to me.

Cowboy Coaches

The coaching staff was led, of course, by Tom Landry. I'd heard that he was cold, hard, and tough and something of a mystery, and my first impression of him didn't do much to dispel that image. I found him very distant and not very caring. He was like a king in terms of power, and peons like the players couldn't insult or anger the king, or they might find themselves on the chopping block. It's true, though, that most of the coaches in the NFL were stern and not overly friendly. The fact is that players are close to a coach or not depending on the plays they make. Players who do well on the field and help the team win usually get more of the coach's positive attention, no matter who they are.

Bob Hayes, who was one of our most notable players, said that Landry was not favorable toward African Americans at that time. I think that appeared in a *Sports Illustrated* interview in 1972 or 1973. While I wouldn't say that Landry didn't want any sort of close relationship with his black players, it's true that he was always a little distant. But as I said, that seemed to be his nature. Whatever the case, Landry definitely was a guy who was sure of himself, and when I looked at the coaches on the Cowboys' defensive side, I could tell that his choices were top-notch in that department. All in all, he was an impressive and excellent leader, and I couldn't help but admire him despite his flaws.

I didn't have any personal contact with Landry until after I started working out, and when it happened, my first interaction wasn't promising. There was a running path that circled the practice facilities, which had earned the nickname the "Cowboy Mile," and we had to run around it as part of our workout. Now, I was fast, quick, and agile, but I'd never been much of a long-distance runner unless I really got in shape and trained for it, partly because of my heart, which had been weakened by my childhood bout of rheumatic fever.

One day in my second week in Dallas, I was jogging around the Cowboy Mile, taking it slow but steady, and Coach Landry, who was out there running, too, came up from behind and passed me. I didn't think much of it, and when I got back to the club room, I went over to work out on the weights with a couple of other guys. While we were working out, Landry walked by, and he paused and said to me, "Don't ever let me pass you again." That was my first conversation with Coach Landry. Later on, I made sure that I passed him when we were both on the trail, and that made him laugh. But I didn't see him laugh much after that, and I quickly noticed that he didn't like to be shown up over anything.

As I said, all the coaches on the defensive side seemed to be pretty good at their jobs. Gene Stallings, who'd been the head coach at Texas A&M, had joined the Cowboys as Landry's secondary coach and defensive coordinator the year before I was drafted to the team. He'd played for Texas A&M, where he was one of the famed Junction Boys under head coach Bear Bryant. In 1956, he helped the A&M win its first Southwest Conference championship since 1939. He was with the Cowboys for fourteen seasons, including their Super Bowl XII win.

I'd never talked to Gene before, though I'd played against A&M a number of times while I was with the Rice Owls, but I was ambivalent about him. He showed himself to be a very pleasant gentleman when I first met him, but it was hard to tell if that was sincere since coaches have to put on a good face when they're recruiting. But I recalled negative comments he'd made in past newspaper articles about black athletes and how he didn't need any. I guess I took those comments personally, so I didn't have a lot of confidence that he and I would get along, and while I didn't hold any ill feeling against him, reservations lingered in the back of my mind. But as I got to know him better, I saw that he was a happy-go-lucky guy who tried to be more hard-nosed than he really was. That probably was from being around Landry. Gene taught lineman technique and let the other coaches coach until Landry got in. Landry pretty much ran the defense himself, so even though Stallings was the defensive back coach, Landry called all the shots on defense.

My linebacker coach was Jerry Tubbs. He'd played middle linebacker for the Cowboys since the beginning of the organization but had retired from playing a few years earlier. He was a quiet, good-hearted man and straightforward when he told you what to do.

Ernie Stautner was the defensive coordinator, which means he ran the whole defense, and he also served as the defensive line coach. Ernie, who'd been born in Germany and emigrated to the US at age three, was a Pro Bowler and Hall of Famer. If you could have packed all his awards into one bundle, it would have been heavy enough to challenge any weight lifter.

On the offensive side, the team had hired "Iron Mike" Ditka just the year before as tight end coach. Ditka had played college and pro ball for years and had been named to both the College Football Hall of Fame and the Pro Football Hall of Fame. He ended his pro career with one season for the Cowboys before taking a coaching job with them, and he was with the Cowboys for nine seasons before going on to serve as head coach for the Chicago Bears and the New Orleans Saints. After that, of course, he became a pro football commentator.

Mike was from Pittsburgh, and while he wasn't racist, in my opinion, he wasn't particularly fond of black players. On top of that, he wasn't a very nice guy. He might have retired from playing, but he still considered himself a player even though he wasn't really big and, by then, was slow and crippled. I don't know how he made the Pro Bowl and all that stuff. I guess he could catch the ball and do what he did. I watched some tapes and films of him playing, and in one game, I saw three or four guys fall off him in cold weather. That probably looked good to the fans, but the truth is, in cold weather, it's harder to tackle. Ditka still had attitude and some fire even if his athletic ability was no longer great, and I think those helped him make it. Even though he was our tight end coach, he always acted like he still wanted to play, and during practice, he frequently suited up and went at it with the players. He also served as an emergency player at tight end even though we already had three tight ends.

Ermal Allen, an older man, was the quarterback coach, working closely with Roger Staubach. He had a heart attack in 1973, but the Cowboys kept him on for another decade.

I think it's fair to say that all the coaches were cautious around Landry, and of course, none of them were black. The only African Americans on the team were players, and there weren't a lot of us—most of us stacked up behind one another, vying for just a couple of positions. There certainly weren't any black quarterbacks, centers, offensive guards, or middle linebackers, though we did have one black left or right linebacker: Ralph Coleman. African Americans were just beginning to come into the picture as tight ends and offensive tackles, but most Black players played defense or wide receiver running back and didn't get a chance to compete against the white players for the choicer positions. At least you didn't see that happening much, and when it did, it was invisible to the public.

The Rookies

As far as the rookie players went, I'd already met Billy Joe DuPree and some of the others in the Blue–Gray game, and I mostly hung out with him and occasionally Drew Pearson and Harvey Martin. DuPree was our first-round tight end, Golden Richards our second-round wide receiver, and Martin our third-round defensive end. All three of them were definitely going to be on the team.

The fourth-round pick was a guy whose name escapes me, but I remember he'd been a defensive back from Tulsa. He'd been a great player all four years of college, and he'd been in the Blue–Gray game, but he never had an opportunity to play pro because he couldn't pass the physical. He had an issue with his heart. I'm not sure what it was, but since I had an enlarged heart from my bout with rheumatic fever, I remained concerned until I passed the physical. I think that he got his signing bonus, but he didn't even get a chance to go to training camp.

Anyway, that kid didn't make it. I hated that happened to him for his own sake, and I also hated it because we needed another defensive back when I was there, and he was a good one. He wouldn't have been the starter in that position, though, since Mel Renfro and Cornell Green—both great players—were in front of him.

In the fifth round, they drafted Bruce Walton, an offensive lineman from UCLA. They brought him in as a tackle. He was a great guy and the older brother of famed basketball player Bill Walton. Then they drafted another offensive guard, Paul Olson, from Illinois or somewhere, in the sixth round. I was, of course, the seventh-round pick, and I've forgotten who was drafted after me.

The Veterans

As we rookies worked out together, we'd see the veterans filter in, but I don't suppose they paid much attention to us. They'd seen a lot of rookies come and go, and nobody knew who was going to make the team, especially those of us way down on the list like I was. The pay we were getting might have been pitiful, but all us rookies were kind of starry-eyed over the veterans because they were the football heroes we'd been watching and hoping to emulate.

The first veteran teammate I met was Bob Lilly, who was playing defensive tackle. Bob, who'd gone to TCU, isn't just a great player with seven All-Pro mentions and eleven Pro Bowl games under his belt. He is just a wonderful man with a good heart—nice and neither crazy nor racist. Physically, he was a big guy, but he was quick and agile and had long arms and large hands that he used to great advantage. He played hard, but by the time I was with the Cowboys, he'd been playing something like ten years and was at the end of his career. His skills, abilities, speed, and reaction time no longer had the edge they once had. But even if he wasn't the Bob of old, so to speak, he was a great guy and a great teammate. No wonder he earned the nickname "Mr. Cowboy" and was the first to have his name inscribed in the Dallas Cowboys' Ring of Honor above Texas Stadium.

Quarterback Roger Staubach also was a great guy as well as one of the most fantastic and famous football players of his era. Maybe that's why he had so many nicknames: Roger the Dodger, Captain America, and Captain Comeback. He attended the US Naval Academy, where he won the Heisman Trophy. Following his service in the Navy, which included a tour of Vietnam, he joined the Cowboys and played his whole pro career for them. That eleven-year span included five Super Bowls with two wins: Super Bowl VI, for which he was named MVP, and Super Bowl XII. He also was a six-time Pro Bowler, and received the NFL Man of the Year Award and—well, I could go on and on about his awards and accolades, but they'd take a whole page, so I'll end with him being given the Presidential Medal of Freedom in 2018. Like I said, Roger was a great guy, but he was feisty, too, and liked to aggravate and provoke you, though that was never over racial issues. He didn't have those like some other people did.

Blaine Nye was at guard, and like Staubach, he played for the Cowboys for his entire pro career. He came from Stanford University, where he was inducted into the Stanford Athletic Hall of Fame as well as being named to the Stanford All-Century football team. By the time he retired from the Cowboys a couple of years after I got there, he'd been a Super Bowl champ and a two-time Pro Bowler.

Ralph Neely was a left offensive tackle. He'd played for the University of Oklahoma, and in 1965, he was chosen by both the Baltimore Colts in the NFL draft and the Houston Oilers in the AFL draft—both in the second round. At first, he went with the Oilers and even accepted their contract offer, but when he learned that the Colts had traded his rights to the Cowboys, he gave the Oilers' advance money back to them and signed with Dallas. That situation resulted in a legal mess that wasn't cleared up until the merger of the AFL and NFL forced a resolution the year after. Like Staubach and Nye, he ended up with the Cowboys for his whole career, though he'd had to take some time off a couple of years before I got there after he broke his left leg in a motorcycle accident.

While Neely was out, Rayfield Wright was moved from tight end to fill his spot. Wright was nicknamed "Big Cat" because he was a big guy but also quick, and by the time I got there, he was already a four-time All-Pro and two-time Pro Bowler. Later, he was a Super Bowl champion and was named to the NFL 1960s All-Decade Team.

And there was Lee Roy Jordan, starting in the position I wanted: middle linebacker. Lee Roy had played for the University of Alabama's Crimson Tide under Paul "Bear" Bryant. He earned MVP for his performance in the Bluebonnet Bowl against the University of Texas Longhorns. He also helped the team to an SEC Championship and a national championship. He also was a member of the College All-Star team that defeated the Green Bay Packers in 1963.

After college, he played exclusively for the Cowboys. Lee Roy wasn't a big guy, only a little over 6' and about 220 pounds, but like Bob Newhouse, he played bigger than he was. In fact, the linebacker lineup of Jordan, Dave Edwards, and Chuck Howley was pure dynamite on the field. Lee Roy would need his own book to list all his achievements and awards, but I will mention that he was the Cowboys' all-time leader in solo tackles. Lee Roy was in solid with the team, and if I was going lay claim to his job, I knew I'd have to play in top form.

The only reason the Cowboys had any visibility at all in the black press was because of Bob Hayes. Bob was just a phenomenal athlete and a multiple Olympic Gold Medalist for the 100-meter sprint and the 4 × 100 meter relay. His leg of that relay is the fastest on record and earned him the title of the fastest human in the world. The press always had stories to tell about Bob, but more important, he's the one who integrated the Cowboys politically, economically, and every other way. Because I'd played a similar role at Rice, I kind of looked at Bob as a larger version of myself—larger because he had so much more experience. He was one of the few players who had any type of exposure beyond hometown life and college athletics. Bob had been all over the world and met people everywhere, so he was more relaxed, self-assured, and able to have fun. Most of the other players were all uptight—most of the black players, for sure—but Bob was just a wonderful man. Nice and kind, he was willing to sit and talk, and you could just kick back, relax, and be yourself with him.

Mel Renfro had been a running back at the University of Oregon. He played safety for the Cowboys for a number of years and was probably the best one in the league, earning himself an All-Pro. He had great speed and could intercept anything that was in the air at any time. The Cowboys probably should have left him in that position, but a couple of years before I got there, Landry moved him to corner.

I'm not sure why Landry did that, but back then, football was basically a running game, though it began to morph into a passing game during the time I was in the league. That meant that the safeties, who usually help the corners with pass coverage, were becoming more prominent. At the time, some teams reserved some positions, such as safety, for white players, relegating black players to the line and a few other less-conspicuous positions. That wasn't the case throughout the league, though. Many other teams weren't so divided and offered choice positions to black players as well as white, but it seemed that the Cowboys weren't that way.

So Landry moved Mel from safety to corner, but talent can't be denied, and Mel proved to be a great corner too. By the end of the 1973 season, he'd chalked up a total of ten Pro Bowls, seven All-Pro mentions, and two Super Bowl appearances. In 1996, he was elected to the Pro Football Hall of Fame. He also was a good guy.

Cornell Green was a five-time Pro Bowler, a three-time first team All-Pro, and a Super Bowl champion. He played catch, meaning he handled the ball like a basketball player. He was playing the left corner, but when Landry moved Mel to right corner, he put Cornell in at strong safety. Landry then put Charlie Waters in at left corner, so while Cornell was covering for Charlie at corner, Mel was playing up on the split end. The results proved what great players Mel and Cornell were because they both made All-Pro in both positions.

Another among the veterans was Chuck Howley. He'd started his tenure with the Cowboys in 1960, and for the first couple of years, he played strong-side linebacker, but in 1963, he moved to weak-side linebacker. The move paid off, and Howley showed himself to be an incredible player. Among his achievements is a record for the second most interceptions—six—by a linebacker in a single season. He was in two NFL championships and two Super Bowls and received a number of awards for his great playing. But by 1973, his career was over, and he only played one game that season, though he suited out and practiced with us. While he still had the skills, speed, and grit, he might not have retained the endurance he once had. Even so, he was still the Cowboys' best linebacker. He was phenomenal, and I really wanted to get to know him and learn from him, but he wasn't sociable at all. He was distant, and he didn't associate with black guys too much anyway. But he was a great player, no doubt. Maybe the best defensive player in the Cowboys' history—certainly the best while I was there. At the time, he'd opened a cleaning and uniform business, and really he was just hanging around in case Landry needed an emergency player.

I also met Bill Thomas, who'd played for Boston College. He was one of four running backs the Cowboys drafted something like three years in a row. Dwayne Thomas was drafted the first of those years, Calvin Hill the second, and both Bill Thomas and Robert Newhouse the third, all in the first or second round. At the time, teams drafted a lot of running backs since pro football was still mainly a running game, and the running backs pretty much carried the load rather than the quarterbacks and receivers. You can imagine the pressure that put on those guys because they'd look around at each other, knowing one or more of them wasn't going to be there very long.

The first black linebacker the Cowboys had was Ralph Coleman. He was from North Carolina A&T University and was drafted the year before I was. He was a good linebacker, and he wore number 56, but pretty soon I inherited his jersey because they ran him out the year I got there. We were in practice one day, and Ralph was going against a tight end—I think it was Mike Ditka, who'd suited up and come out during practice. Landry said something to Ralph, and Ralph said something back to Landry, and the next thing we knew, Ralph was out of there. Ralph was a good player, but as I've already noted, Landry was extremely sensitive to anything he took to be criticism or defiance. If you challenge someone like that, what do you think he's going to do? The bottom line is that if you're going to be critical of your boss, you'd better do it on the side, one-on-one, and figure out a way to communicate properly, instead of doing it in public.

The thing about football is, it's a rough, tough, macho game. When you put on that suit and go out on that field, you're not the same guy you are walking down the street. To survive on the gridiron, you have to put on a whole different demeanor along with that suit. Ralph was out there practicing, and practicing hard, and trying to do what he needed to do. He wasn't fighting against anybody or trying to fight Landry, but harsh words can be said when you're in those types of situations and are maybe a little worked up. And Landry was so sensitive that you couldn't say anything to him. So when Ralph did, that was the end of Ralph, who didn't even make it to the beginning of the season. The stated reason for the separation was that Ralph and the team couldn't come to an agreement on playing time and pay. Having seen it all go down, I should have smelled a rat then, but that odor was to come on strong later. I thought Ralph was a cool guy, but that was pretty much it for his pro career. After that, his life took a real downward spiral.

Robert Newhouse was another who played for Dallas his entire careers. He was drafted the year before me, and I already knew him since he'd played for the University of Houston, Rice's hometown rivals. In a remarkable career at UH, he finished as the school's all-time leading rusher, and many of the school records he set remain standing today. In the pros, he was an excellent running back, but when he was switched from that to fullback, he did well and eventually replaced Walt Garrison after Walt retired. At 5'10" and only a little over 200 pounds, Bob was small for pro football, but his spirit made him seem larger. His low-to-the-ground build and tremendous lower-body power earned him the nickname "the Human Bowling Ball," and he used his strength to great advantage to lead the Cowboys in rushing. The Cowboys went to three Super Bowls while Bob was with them, winning Super Bowl XII in 1977. After his retirement, he was inducted into the Texas Black Sports Hall of Fame. Unfortunately, failing health took its toll on him, and he succumbed to heart disease in 2014.

Calvin Hill, who was two or three years older than me, went to Yale University, where he earned a divinity degree. He mostly played halfback for Yale, and thanks to him and quarterback Brian Dowling, the school had an undefeated season his rookie year. He also was a Yale track-and-field star and holds the school record for the outdoor triple jump. After college, he was a first-round draft pick by the Cowboys, who put him in as linebacker and tight end but eventually settled him in as running back. Calvin excelled in that position and was considered the best in the league for a time. He was not only the first Cowboy running back to rush for more than 1,000 yards in a single season (1972), he also was the second to do so the next year. Unfortunately, he suffered several injuries during a couple of years' span, which halted his momentum. But he was back in form after that and helped the Cowboys win Super Bowl VI and two NFC titles. He also went to four Pro Bowls and was named to two All-Pro teams.

Calvin's personal life is just as interesting as his pro career. He's a preacher thanks to his divinity degree from Yale, and the school also gave him an honorary doctorate in 2016. He's the father of NBA player Grant Hill, and he has served on the boards of directors for the Baltimore Orioles and several other organizations. Perhaps more important, from my standpoint, he serves as a consultant to pro sports teams, specializing in working with troubled players. That's certainly the kind of person I needed when I was in the pros.

We had a great wide receiver that year in Otto Stowe, who'd played for Iowa State University. He was a second-year player we picked up during my rookie year in a trade with the Miami Dolphins, where he'd been a second-round draft choice. Don Schula decided to get rid of him for some reason. We traded him out for the original number 88, Ron Sellers. I know that Drew Pierson later called himself the original number 88, but Ron Sellers was the real original number 88. Otto was a couple of inches over 6' and very handsome. More to the point for the Cowboys, he also was an excellent receiver. He had great hands and didn't drop anything. He was very quick and had great moves and all that. But when he came to camp, Landry got upset with him over lifting weights. Stowe said lifting weights hurt his back, which of course didn't satisfy Landry. When Otto broke his ankle in the seventh game of the season against the Philadelphia Eagles and went on the injured list, that was all the excuse Landry needed to get rid of him. At the end of the season, Landry traded Otto to the Denver Broncos. That really disappointed me because I'd made friends with Otto, and we scrimmaged together and worked out after practice, going one-on-one, with me trying to cover him. I never did intercept or stop him, though I might have blocked passes a couple of times.

Mike Montgomery took over Otto's job, but he broke his leg in the very next game. The next guy up was Drew Pearson, and that's how Drew got to play. He was actually a third-string wide receiver, and his stellar career shows the kinds of good things that can happen for a team if motivated players are given a chance to shine.

Anyway, there we rookies were, watching all those cool guys come in and knowing that most of them were pretty good football players. And the situation on the team was equally cool. No matter where you are, you have to adapt yourself to the social and cultural norms around you, and we all know how it is in the South. But that didn't negatively affect everyone. Guys like Staubach, Lilly, John Fitzgerald, Blaine Nye, Charlie Waters, and Cliff Harris didn't have a lot of racial issues, and as for those who did, fortunately, they didn't openly display their animosity as strongly as did the Dallas community around us. As for the few who did show negative racial behavior at times, well, it's professional sports, so it is what it is. You just have to ignore that kind of stuff as best as you can and move on.

That didn't mean there weren't divisions within the team, but mostly they were natural divisions. The offense didn't hang out with the defense too much, for example, because the two teams met and practiced at different times. The main times the defense and offense associated was on the special teams. Almost all the rookies were involved in the special teams, one way or another. Not DuPree, though, since he was going to be a starting tight end. And as I recall, they put Golden Richards behind Bob Hayes. Harvey Martin was over on the left side, trying to play left defensive end, but he ended up being on the right side, playing right defensive end.

That's what I was doing just before we went to training camp: working out and getting to know and engaging with all those guys. I think that, at the time, the Cowboys carried only forty-three players or so—ten fewer than they carry now. But underneath everything lay the fact that our contracts were pretty much day-to-day. Any of us— veteran as well rookie—could get cut at any moment, and we were witnessing cuts happening right in front of us, like Ralph Coleman. That put a subtle yet constant strain on everyone.

Practice

As I met the coaches, some of the scouts, and the players, everything seemed okay for the moment. Even though I'd had that little thing with Landry while running the Cowboy Mile, I wasn't too worried. I hadn't been drafted until the seventh round, but I knew I could play, and I figured that with my talent, hard work, and success on the field, I'd have no problem making the team. But I found out the hard way that not everything was legit in the NFL. Pro football is a business, and in any business, there are three components: a product, an organization, and politics. And it's the politics that really hurts sports because it often leads away from the truth, and the truth of football lies in the performance on the field and in those who can perform.

As is obvious from Ralph Coleman's all-too-brief career, it's not just what you're doing, because you can do well and still get cut in the NFL. I didn't know that at the time. I thought that if you played well, you were in. Or somebody else would pick you up. But the NFL, as well as teams, could blackball you and all that stuff, though I wasn't yet aware of the extent they would go to destroy players they didn't like for any reason—sometimes for no real reason at all but personal pique.

But I was quickly learning that the NFL is a very political organization, with different levels to those politics that go way beyond the day-to-day stresses the players are under. Basically, sports is entertainment. It's putting on a show, and for Landry, the stars of the show weren't the players, the guys the fans were coming—and paying—to see. As far as Landry was concerned, the stars were himself, the other coaches, and the owners. The players were just faceless names in Cowboy uniforms. That was, in fact, almost literally true. When

I played for the Cowboys, nobody was supposed to know what we looked like, and we weren't allowed to take off our helmets or show our faces. The only things the fans knew about us were our names, numbers, and how well we played.

On top of all that, black players had to face the rampant racial bigotry in Dallas. Playing for the Cowboys was great, and so were most of my teammates, but playing while black in Dallas at that time was terrible. In terms of living conditions and being able to grow and develop and have opportunities, Dallas just wasn't there. In college, many of us found racial truth—if not harmony—through knowledge, skills, attitude, and personal character. But when we got out of college, all that stuff vanished as society's norms reinstated themselves and dominated culture, associations, activities, and personal development— dominated everything.

The situation was better in some places, worse in others. Houston was a big country town that had grown into a city, and if you had money and were cool, people didn't mind racial differences so much. I never had a problem driving around Houston, but a lot of people in Dallas didn't like to see black men riding around in expensive cars and enjoying themselves. They wanted us working with our heads down. Just driving down a Dallas street could see me getting stopped by police for no reason.

America might have integrated, but in Dallas, that was just for show. The city was just about 100 percent redneck, and they didn't like black people. Even finding a decent place to live could be a challenge. Ralph Neely, for example, had bought some apartments in Dallas, and he rented one to Mel Renfro. But Mel was forced to move after the residents complained about having a black man living in the complex. And a lot of African Americans wouldn't take a chance on crossing the invisible racial line because, whether out of fear or complacency, they didn't want the heat it would bring down on them.

That didn't mean all African Americans took the situation sitting down. The city had to deal with black athletes because some of the guys—like Bob Hayes—were so well-known. Bob was a big man and famous, and they couldn't mess with him much. So as a pro athlete, I had some privileges. It was kind of like being in college, where your position helps buffer you from the outside world. I moved from my small apartment to the seventeenth floor of a high-rise apartment building on Preston Road. No black man had done that before in Dallas, but no one had tried.

So I integrated the building, and it' management treated me right, but outside on the streets of Dallas, it was a challenge just to stand up and ask for respect and due process. Doing that could get you killed, and white cops were killing blacks, just like they still do some places today. Society allows them to do that because killing black people doesn't have any real consequences or effect on society, so lots of people don't care.

But such acts do affect entire communities and raise whole ranges of issues—from personal safety to childhood development to economic and cultural opportunities. In the end, society as a whole is threatened by that kind of behavior. The legal system frequently tests us—and society—and after living in Dallas for just a short while, I quickly caught on that the tests are often rigged—at least for minorities.

So there I was. In Dallas. It was like going back in time even while I worked hard to move into a future on the team and find some enjoyment in life. But the middle of July rolled around quickly enough, and the racial tensions of Dallas faded into the background as we flew off to training camp.

CHAPTER

9

THOUSAND OAKS

Training camp was near Los Angeles, and I flew in about a week early so I could spend some time with my dad, who lived in Compton. Except for his brief appearance at my graduation, I hadn't seen him in something like thirteen years, and I wanted to try to reestablish our relationship. We hung out together during that week and kicked it around a little bit. I also met his wife, her son, Tab, from a previous marriage, and their son together, Jock. Even though Jock was my brother by blood, I didn't know anything about him, so it was good meeting him. He was a little shy at first, but he loosened up some, and we had a chance to talk about things.

A few days that week before camp started, I went over to UCLA to work out, and while I was there, I met O. J. Simpson and Bubba Smith. I already knew Bubba's brother, Toby, who'd been drafted by the Cowboys a couple of years earlier. I also met a few basketball players, such as Cheek Willis and a couple of star players for UCLA. We not only worked out at the facilities but also ran some plays. Once early on while I was talking to OJ, he called me "old man." I told him I was only twenty-three, and he said, "Naw, you can't be in your twenties. You look like you're in your thirties." Maybe he thought that because I was already losing my hair. Whatever the reason, he referred to me as the "Old Man" after that even though I was a rookie and only a few years younger than he was. After workouts, though, I didn't hang out with any of those guys. I might have, but nobody was asking, so I'd just go back to Dad's house and spend time with him and his family.

When the week was up, I moved to the Cowboys' training camp, which was at California Lutheran College in Thousand Oaks, twenty or so miles from Malibu. Back then, the team was there for about five weeks, and during our stay, we lived in the college dorms. Most of us at camp that first week were rookies, though the veterans who weren't starting showed up too.

On the very first day, we had to run a mile in quarters—four times around the track. It was a test of our physical condition. We'd run one quarter, have a few seconds of rest, then run the next, and so on until the end. Each position had to run the distance in a particular time. As a linebacker prospect, I had to run each quarter in seventy-eight seconds, with a thirty-second rest between each quarter. I made it through the first three, but by the time I was coming down the home stretch of the fourth quarter, I was worn out and could barely go on. I'd never been much of a distance runner, and although I had moments where I could manage it, it wasn't something I could do at will on a regular basis.

As I came down the home stretch, I had to stop sprinting and came in at a jog. Some of the other guys started yelling at me to push harder, but I couldn't. I was frustrated and mad, and all I could say to them was, "I ain't no track star. I'm a football player." Some of the guys laughed, but I noticed Landry looking at me in a way that said he wasn't amused—and he shouldn't have been. I just forgot about it, though. I might not have made my required time, but while the other guys reached the finish line at a sprint, I don't think any of them actually made their times, either.

When I couldn't pass my test run, the coaches thought I wasn't in shape and had me do three-a-days—mostly conditioning—for the rest of the week. I'd come in early for a workout, then do our regular workout in late morning and another in midafternoon. After that, I had to do some more running. I didn't take offense or complain about any of it since all that work just made me quicker, stronger, and better prepared.

In fact, Landry tested me quite a bit during my time in camp, not only to see if I was strong and tough enough to endure being attacked by guys play after play but also to gauge my temperament and dedication. But I held up. I'd been through some tough stuff during my three years of play in the Southwest Conference, and I proved myself to Landry's satisfaction, at least regarding my ability to play.

Every weekend, we'd have a scrimmage, and like many of the rookies, I regularly scrimmaged with the veterans. That first week or two, we scrimmaged against our own teammates, but toward the end of camp, we scrimmaged with the LA Rams and San Francisco 49ers. When we had an internal scrimmage, our first-string offense would go against the second-string defense, and the second-string offense played against the first-string defense. That meant that those of us on the second teams were playing tough, experienced guys. But in a sense, it also meant that we weren't practicing our own game. A lot of times during practice, when you face off against your own offensive line, you don't play in your own style of defense. Instead, you try to imitate the style of play of the guy the offensive player in front of you will have to face during the game. You learn that opponent's style by watching film or tape of his games to see how he plays. There's a good reason to do this: playing in the style of your opponent better prepares your offense to deal with the opponent's strengths and exploit his weaknesses.

In my first scrimmage, we were practicing in full uniforms. I did very well, but it proved, in a sense, to be my personal test. The rest of the veterans had come in, and we were rotating for scrimmage, so I got to run a play with them. In my first play, the defensive line was Bob Lilly, Jethro Pugh, Pat Toomay, and Larry Cole. Dave Edwards was at the strong-side linebacker position, Lee Roy Jordan in the middle, and Chuck Howley at the weak side, though D. D. Lewis was coming up and would eventually take Howley's position after he retired.

We ran the scrimmage play, and Calvin Hill got the ball and was headed toward the goal. So I ran at Calvin, but just as I got to him, he broke stride for just a second. When he did that, I made the mistake of hesitating before I went in to hit him. I only hesitated a split second, but that was enough time for Bob, Lee Roy, and Chuck—all big guys—to reach us. There I was, right in the middle, as they slammed into Calvin and me, *bang, bang, bang*. It was like a freight train crash, and when it was all over, I got up, checking myself—my limbs, my head, my body—to make sure I was still in one piece.

Then I had to check my mind and resolve.

Wow, I thought, *you sure you want to do this? This isn't any kiddie game. This is the real deal.* And it had all been so fast and very intimidating with all that speed, size, and strength coming right at me. I had to stand there for a moment, deciding if I could take that kind of punishment on a regular basis. When all those seasoned linemen start coming at you, you'd better be ready for it. Right then and there, I developed a lot of respect for running backs because those guys have to run into that stuff all the time. Guys like that have to be tough and have their minds really made up to do something like that, especially since a lot of them get popped pretty good once or twice in their careers.

That was my first significant experience with football at the pro level, and after I realized I was still in one piece, I made up my mind to stick with it and go for the goal. A lot of the other younger guys couldn't handle it, though, and some of them didn't even wait to get cut. They knew they couldn't take it, and they'd just pack up and leave in the middle of the night. But I had to take it because I vowed not to quit. I knew I'd have to give 100 percent, and when I did, I lit up my opposition. After about two weeks of that, I was thinking, *Hey, I can handle this.* The second week, we moved into our regular practice schedule. Each day, we had

practice, a break, meeting, practice, a break, meeting, then another meeting. Day in and day out, that's what we did: going through the playbook, learning the defense, and running the plays. As an individual, you have to put all that stuff into your mind and body thoroughly and indelibly because when you're facing an opponent on the field, you have to make decisions and act on them in an instant, all while using maximum effort. It seems simple enough on paper, but no matter which side of the line you're on—offense or defense—you have eleven guys who have to coordinate with each other, and that's what makes it so complex.

Getting down the moves and the timing so that everyone and everything functions well is absolutely necessary. Everybody has to be on the same page at the same time, and part of that is learning how to read the offense formation you're defending against so you can figure out which plays are most likely. And sometimes that page has to be turned quickly to defeat the ability of your opponents to read your own intentions through your positioning or team line-up. You often see teams moving offensive as well as defensive players around before the ball is snapped, trying to confuse the other team. Then after the ball is snapped, changes happen fast, and everybody has to coordinate and change at the same time. That might require altering position or changing attack, but whatever happens, everybody has to be on point and able to make the right moves on the fly. If one person is off, it throws everything off, and your opponents are going to score.

There also is the matter of reading not just the formations on the other side of the scrimmage line but the individual players too. That's why being a veteran helps because those guys are experienced and have seen it before, while rookies have to go through it all to recognize what's happening. When you're playing against certain players, for example, it might take you two or three games to learn how to approach them based on your mutual skills. I had speed and some strength, so I had an advantage if I didn't let the big guys get me at the beginning. If the guys on the line are doing their jobs, then the backfield players can bring their personal skills into play.

At first, you don't know anything about any of that because you're a rookie, and learning takes time. But I was catching on, learning to read the quarterbacks and the different formations, and I worked hard to get the plays down in my head and on the field. One element I concentrated on was my pass return, which needed some work. I'd been pretty good at it in college ball, but in the pros, it's a little different because there's a lot of trickery and other stuff going on. Landry kept playing me in all three linebacker positions: weak side, strong side, and middle. My weakest position was the strong side because I didn't have the size or long arms, and I was facing tight ends who were taller and heavier than me. In cases like that, I'd always have to cheat a little bit—either in my stance or on my first move—in order to defend my territory. The weak side, however, facing the split end, I could handle with my eyes closed. The middle wasn't any problem either. I loved it. I was like a star running back in the middle. If my linemen did what they were supposed to do, I could clean up. And I brought some force with it. Running backs didn't want to see me coming. If they tried to run over me, I'd make them fumble, and if they tried something else,

I'd tear them up. One way or another, I was going to get them. I was young, spirited, and going hard.

While all this was happening and I was building up my game, sportscasters started taking an interest in me. I guess they were impressed with my playing, and when they interviewed me, I brashly told them that I hadn't come to sit on the bench. I was there to start as middle linebacker. That's what I'd done everywhere I'd played, though really, my focus at the time was on making the team. My statements shocked everybody, of course. Lee Roy was good, and he had a great year that ended in a Pro Bowl, yet here I was, some rookie upstart laying claim to his job.

But for me, it was just a statement of fact because that middle linebacker position was what I wanted. I wasn't playing to get rich. I was playing because I liked playing football and wanted to do it. I figured I was good for seven or eight years, since after about age thirty, you start declining. Football is a strong young man's game, and I was realistic about my ability to last as a top-notch player.

If I got the chance to play.

Interference

Landry heard about what I'd said, of course, and on the third week of camp, he called me into his office.

"Rodrigo," he told me, "you're not going to start in middle linebacker."

I said, "What?" He repeated himself, and I said, "Well, Coach, that's what I'm here for. I'm here to compete, and I think I can take this job. I haven't seen Lee Roy do anything I can't do. And I can do stuff he can't." Landry gave me a funny look and was adamant. "I'm just trying to let you know," he said, "that you're not going to start as middle linebacker." If I was interested in starting, he said, I should consider another position, such as weak-side linebacker.

I heard him, but throughout my life, I'd often had people tell me what I wasn't able to do, and I'd learned to ignore those sorts of claims on my desires and life. Landry's mind was set, as was often the case with people who told me those sorts of things, but despite that, I still intended to start as middle linebacker. So I said to him, "Okay, Coach.

I hear what you're saying, and I respect your opinion and you're the coach. But I'm not going at it like that. I'm going to be what I'm trying to be."

I had no choice but to ignore Landry's refusal to let me start at middle linebacker. In order for me to stay focused and do my best, I had to approach the game and my position in it from my own standpoint. When I went into pro sports, my belief was that the best guy was going to play. But after Landry refused me the position, I had to awaken to the fact that skill and ability weren't necessarily deciding factors in pro sports. We rookies trusted and respected our organization, but I learned right then that the trust and respect were not reciprocal. That was a foreign notion to me. I was a guy who made things happen on the field, and I couldn't understand—or maybe I didn't want to understand— Landry's refusal. The truth is that Landry was used to putting people on the shelf and doing what he wanted with them, and even though I was somewhat demanding, he wouldn't give in. Eventually his hardness worked against him, and he began to lose players because of it. A couple of years later, when Thomas "Hollywood" Henderson came in, Landry gave him everything—let him start and paid him well—because by then Landry needed good players, and he had to treat them better. That state of affairs benefitted Hollywood a great deal, and he proved to be a great player. He inherited the number I wore while I was with the Cowboys.

So even though Landry kept saying that I wasn't going to start, I either didn't listen or didn't pay attention because my mind was set on what I was trying to do and what I was there to play for. Like I said, it wasn't for the money. For someone at my level, pro football wasn't paying a lot. It might have been different if they were paying me a couple of hundred thousand a year, but that first year, they paid me less than $40,000 once you factored in salary, signing bonus, and incentives. It wasn't great money. If I was going to put my life and well-being on the line, I thought, then it better be for something that I like and want to do. Nor was it about fame and popularity. I didn't care about those. That wasn't me. Besides, it was the 1970s, and I was black. How much fame and popularity was I going to have anyway? What I did have was my powerful desire to play football in the starting middle linebacker position. But Lee Roy Jordan already had that job, so what were they going to do with me?

Maybe more important was what was I going to do? I was stubborn, and in many ways, I thought I had some light while remaining totally in the dark. I knew what I wanted, but I was out on a limb, both psychologically and emotionally. Football is a very proud, macho sport, and so your mentality is going to have a macho combativeness and cockiness that can hurt you if you're not aware of what you're dealing with. The fact is that life isn't always about the fight or the battle but about what's best, what's the right thing to do in order to move on. You have to be clear about why you are in a particular situation, what the real objective is, where you are, and how you can achieve your objective.

If, for example, you sue somebody, all you can get are rights, privileges, or money. If you don't understand that, then you can get caught up in other things driven more by ego than anything that's real or true. You might want to stand up and prove what's right, but when you're prideful, issues become something other than what they actually are. When you sue somebody, it's not about what's right. It's about the money or other tangible outcome. Either you're going to win or you're not, and if you do win, it's the money you're taking home, not anything else. It's that simple, but when you're young and self-important, you can't see things clearly.

So I was dealing with all that external stuff, and the issues and problems they caused were only compounded by problems my pride created for me in that culture and environment. At the same time, I was trying to figure out how I was going to make it in pro football. I felt that I had a shot to show my talents and go for what I wanted, but that wasn't so. I hadn't yet realized how prejudiced and backward the NFL was. The attitudes of some of the white coaches and others toward minorities was just way out there. I was surprised that the coaches looked on players, no matter what race, as if they were nothing. "I can get another one tomorrow" was the unspoken statement in their attitudes.

I didn't know anything about that at first, but I quickly saw that when you're a star for the team, you might have all these people telling you you're all right even if you're not. And all the while, they're looking for the next new star, so you'd better get yours while you can and move on. In the beginning, I expected fairness, but there wasn't any of that. If you really want to succeed in pro sports, then you do what the coaches tell you to do, but it seemed to me that there wasn't enough money in the game for me to constantly bow down to authority. Besides, bowing down wasn't the kind of thing I was good at. I was a competitor, a hard worker, and a stand-up guy. Those were the qualities I valued and could be comfortable with.

I was living and learning at the same time, and when I had challenges or had to figure out what to do next, I often made bad decisions. And I don't mean little mistakes. I thought I was right, but I was wrong. Sometimes I was focused on things that didn't need focusing on, but a lot of times, I just didn't see issues for what they were. I was making so many mistakes and creating so many problems that it looked like everywhere I turned was really the wrong direction. I can truthfully say that there weren't too many decisions that I made in my twenties that were correct. I wasn't trying to be a bad person; it was just that I was blowing it and ruining my own life. Instead of listening, waiting, or exercising restraint, I let my pride, lust, and impatience take over.

Another part of the equation was that I simply didn't understand the cost of just trying to maneuver. One of my bad decisions was to act as my own agent and manager. The league had never seen that sort of thing from anyone, much less a black player, and they surely weren't going to let that float. It was definitely the wrong approach in the NFL at that time if you wanted to skate by. Sometimes you're lucky or you're such a great athlete or person that you can do that, but that wasn't me. I was the kind of guy who always faced problems head on, though I didn't approach problems by going into a situation and demand that people give me something I hadn't earned. Too often in life, though, people don't want to play the game fairly. They won't give you anything—not even an opportunity. And because nobody was giving me anything, and there was no one behind me cheerleading, I usually had to go into a situation, metaphorically kick butt, and take mine. So while I was used to having problems, I didn't realize that just being me could be a problem in itself.

Throughout all this, I still didn't have anyone to confide in and bounce things off—someone who truly cared and who had knowledge enough to say, "Look at this" or "Focus on that." I was the type of person who did fine when I was focused on what I supposed to be doing, but trying to call the shots in areas in which I had no experience proved disastrous. I thought I had a little knowledge, but like they say, a little knowledge is a dangerous thing.

Ironically, though, while I wanted guidance, my terrible situation was made worse by the fact that no one could tell me very much of anything because I wouldn't listen and was very defensive. When you're like that, you miss out on a lot of information because you're not even listening and are very combative, even in your thinking. At a time when I really need mentorship, I made the tremendous mistake of refusing to listen to anyone.

Basically, I had a lack of trust. It was as if everybody had ulterior motives when they told me things, so when people tried to guide me, I didn't listen because I couldn't trust what anybody said. It could have been that those who really tried to help me also had ulterior motives, but that didn't mean that they weren't sincere in their efforts to guide me toward a better path. But once you get into a mindset of mistrust—maybe with a little fear that you might mess up mixed in—then disaster is going to come. You might be playing well on the field, but what about after you leave the field and put on your street clothes? Where's life? What do you want to do, and where do you want to go? And you look around for answers, but everything seems so fake, and people want to use you. So you really don't know who's giving you the straight story and who's feeding you a line.

Not having someone to explain things and remind me what this was all about—what the real objective was and where I could actually go—led me to get easily carried away. I thought, *I'm going to do this, and I'm going to make this right, and I'm going to stand here*, but none of that was at all important. That's what I struggled with in my twenties, and I fouled up and wasted a lot of time and effort messing with the wrong people or the wrong issues. When I think about it now, it makes me a little angry at myself, but really it was just sad that I wasted so much of my time and energy like that.

Something that most young folks, like I was at the time, haven't learned is that the ramifications of bad decisions can last for years—for me, all the way into my thirties. Once you make one of those bad moves, it's not something you can easily recover from, if at all. I can only praise the Lord God that he kept me afloat because everybody else just got out of the way to see if I was going to sink or not. And none of them were throwing me a life raft or anything. Guys who have a wife or loyal girlfriend or some money might get a little support, but that wasn't me. Life is real, and since I didn't have any help, I knew I'd have to stay afloat on my own. So things were really rough for me psychologically and emotionally even though things looked pretty good on the outside.

Many of these realizations had yet to come to me, of course. There I was, a twenty-three-year-old Dallas Cowboy draftee in training camp, fulfilling a lifelong dream, so I didn't yet perceive my situation as other than an opportunity—an opportunity for fun as well as work. Several weeks in training camp is a long time for macho young guys to go without female companionship. Down in Thousand Oaks, school was out, but some of the women students remained in town, and some of the guys went out with them. But for a lot of us, making the team took up most of our time.

At first, nobody took much notice of me, but after about three weeks of training camp, I was doing well, and some of the veterans started talking to me. Craig Martin, Walt Garrison, and a few of the other guys were going to a couple of clubs in Malibu, and I rode along and hung out with them. At that time, Malibu wasn't fenced in with gated communities like it is today. I was the only black player there. I met some chicks and James Garner and other movie stars. We did this a few weekends, and even though curfew was at 11:00 p.m., we'd come in late—something like 2:00 a.m. Since I was riding with them, I had no choice but to break curfew, and I was scared.

"Man," I told them, "I don't need to be cut for staying out late." They weren't worried and just came back to the dorms, laughing and making noise, while I'd be creeping and sneaking in like a guilty mouse. Well, nobody "caught" me. The coaches knew what was going on and tolerated it, but I didn't know that.

To my surprise, sometimes I'd be creeping in, only to run into other guys sneaking out. Those were usually the ones who called it quits, packed up their suitcases, and were going home. It was just another way to get cut. We had 130 or 140 rookies that year. Back then, teams could bring in as many rookies as they wanted. Now they bring in something like ninety. I don't know why the numbers were so high, because the management was wasting a lot of time and resources coaching a bunch of guys who'd just vanish into the night. I guess, though, that every once in a while, you can find a diamond in the rough, and in the end, it didn't cost the teams too much since they were barely paying rookies a living wage.

Preseason Games

After about three weeks of scrimmaging, we prepared to begin our preseason schedule. The preseason games give the coaches a chance to see their players in action, though by then, about half the players had left or been cut. For most teams, there are four preseason games unless you also play in the Pro Football Hall of Fame Game, in which case you play five. The Hall of Fame Game is usually the first of the preseason games, and that year, the New England Patriots played the San Francisco 49ers, who won 20–7.

Our first two preseason games were against the Oakland Raiders and the LA Rams while we were still out on the West Coast. Bob Lilly sat out both games. It wasn't unusual for the veterans to do that, especially the super players, and Bob and Lee Roy were two of the best in the league at that time. For one thing, we didn't get paid for preseason games. I guess the veterans figured it wasn't worth the effort to play without pay, especially since they could get hurt just as easily in a preseason game as in the Super Bowl. But I saw it as an opportunity because it gave me the chance to start as weak-side linebacker.

We played the Raiders first, but the day didn't start out well. I overslept and was late for breakfast, so I was fined. It was only something like $50, but as I've said, I wasn't getting paid all that much, and even $50 hurt. But the day got better. Lee Roy started the game as middle linebacker, and at first, the Raiders tried to run the ball using sweeps around the left tackle. After a few plays, Lee Roy complained about a minor injury, and Landry called me to the side.

"Can you stop them from running the sweep?" he asked. I'd seen the play before and thought I could.

"Yes, sir," I said, and he told me to go in there and do it.

It was great that Landry was giving me a chance at middle linebacker, but all week, he'd been practicing me as weak-side linebacker, and when you're playing defense, it's best to play the position you practice. You've spent weeks honing your skills in that position, and that leaves you a little cold if you're suddenly shifted elsewhere. I don't know if it was true in this case, but Landry would do stuff like that to break you down. In football, the coaches and management do their best to break you down psychologically and turn you into a machine.

Considering who I was facing in this game, maybe I had to be a machine. Right in front of me was the Raiders' All-Pro center, Jim Otto, and behind him was quarterback Ken Stabler, another fantastic player. To his left were Art Shell at tackle and Gene Upshaw at guard, both also All-Pros. And to the right were Bob Brown and several other great players. So there I was, a rookie playing middle linebacker against a team made up of legends of the game. But I couldn't dwell on that because it was time to play.

So I went in, but it was no easy thing. Otto was getting up tight on the line, and at 6'2" and 255 pounds, he was nothing to sneer at, and neither were the other Raiders' linemen, many of whom were close to 300 pounds. I was only 225, so I had to work to take away the angles and give them their nose to be effective. We stopped them a few times, but it was tough trying to get out on pass plays while also covering if they tried to run a counter.

During the game, Harvey Martin was sent in as left defensive end facing All-Pro, All-World Bob "Boomer" Brown. Bob was probably the best offensive tackles in the NFL partly because of his size: about 6'4" and 280 pounds. During the game, he had both his hands heavily wrapped up in tape so that his thumbs were protected but sticking out. The ball was snapped, and it was a pass play, so I dropped back to see where the receiver was going and so forth. And what I saw when I glanced over at Harvey amazed me. Bob had hooked his protruding thumbs up into the sides of Harvey's rib cage, hoisted him off the ground, and was shaking him in the air. Now, Harvey was nearly as tall as Bob, and though he weighed a lot less, he was still a big guy and not used to being picked up at all. Then Bob slammed Harvey to the turf and dove right on top of him. When I saw that, I thought, *Whoo-ee. This ain't no playing. This is some real stuff.*

Then Bob got up, shook himself a little, and walked to his own huddle, leaving Harvey lying there on the ground. It's no easy thing to have that kind of weight slammed down on you like that, and I stared at Harvey, thinking he had to be dead. His helmet was twisted half around on his head, making it look like his neck was broken. Then I saw his nose poking through his earhole and knew his head hadn't twisted around with the helmet. A moment later, he staggered to his feet, and all I could think was, *Thank God, he's intact.* Harvey was a strong, proud man, but when I looked in his eyes, what I saw there was, "Good God, what just happened to me?" I mean, no one had ever picked him up and slammed him down like that.

Then we lined up for the next play, and Harvey and Bob faced off again, and I was thinking I really wanted to see what happened next. But when their quarterback called the snap, instead of charging Bob like he was supposed to do, Harvey sidestepped toward the sideline and avoided direct contact. Now Harvey was a great football player, but I guess he wasn't about to have Bob pick him up and throw him down again. Every player gets hit on the field, and most of the time, it's not all that bad. But when you have those big moments and are hit hard, you have to regroup and get yourself back together. Then you have to decide whether you can take the hits or not, and that might have been one of Harvey's deciding points. He must have decided right and gotten over his fear because after that, he went on, played hard, and became an NFL superstar. Nobody could block Harvey one-on-one. They had to double-team him.

As for me, I just went in there and ran hard and did my best, and even though we lost the game, I appreciated that Landry gave me the opportunity to play middle linebacker—especially since it was my first chance to play against big-time pro opponents.

Our second game was against the Rams, and Landry did the same thing to me, only reversed: he practiced me on in the middle but played me on the outside. And I wasn't the only one. Although we made a few plays against the Rams, we fell behind because too many of us were playing positions we hadn't practiced. And the coaches weren't always making the right decisions. One time, they told me to attack the running back to turn him to the outside. It wasn't the right thing to do to get me in the correct position to be effective, but I did like they said.

When it didn't work out to Landry's satisfaction, he got upset with me even though I was just following instructions. And when the other coaches wouldn't stand up for me, I learned right then that nobody was going to take responsibility for telling me to do something that Landry didn't like.

Making the Cut

After that, we flew back to Dallas. As we boarded the bus to leave the college where we'd been staying, all those young ladies who'd been going out with the players for the last month or so came out to tell them goodbye. It was funny watching a lot of the guys ducking and hiding and trying to sneak onto the bus to keep from running into some local girl who wanted to lay claim to him. We all laughed at—and with—one another over that.

It's not there anymore, but back then, there was a Ramada Inn on the Central Expressway. We stayed there for a week or two while we finished our preseason games and, more to the point for many of us, waited to find out who'd survive the final cut. While we stayed there, we also got to know one another better. And then there were all the young ladies coming through, wanting to meet Cowboys. You could call them football groupies, I guess, so there were a few distractions at the hotel even though Landry tried his best to run them off.

Somebody else Landry ran off was a guy who'd been a supporter of mine while I'd been with the Rice Owls. The guy visited me, and he'd figured out that I was going to make the team because of what people were saying and what I'd showed myself capable of in practice. Landry noticed him and asked me who he was. I told him he was a guy I'd known back in Houston. Landry didn't say anything more about it at that moment, but a couple of days later, he came up to me and said, "You need to stay away from that guy. I don't want him hanging around."

Landry had done a background check on him and thought he was involved in gambling and underworld activity. That might have been so, though I don't really know. When I was in Houston, I didn't just hang out at Rice. I got around the city's hot spots, like Market Square and Dowling Street, where I met all sorts of people whose backgrounds

I knew nothing about. I was a young, spirited, and adventurous guy from the streets of Waco, and I wasn't going to limit myself, so I did the streets in Houston. But I never let myself get too involved in what I saw going on around me. In some ways, I was more interested in the women and in observing my surroundings. The guy in question had been good to me back then, but thanks to Landry, I caught on that he was a little shady and probably was going to try to get some insider information from me. I'm not sure, but that incident might have further affected Landry's opinion of me.

Our third preseason game—and first home game—was against the Kansas City Chiefs, and Lee Roy Jordan sat out that one. He took off a week because of a minor injury, but he was a great player and thought he was worth more than the Cowboys were paying him, so maybe he was angling for more money too. Bob Lilly and a few of the other guys were trying to get more money as well. Because Lee Roy sat out that game, Landry said he was going to start me in middle linebacker. *Yeah,* I thought, *now I can prove my stuff.*

One day after practice, I went into the shower to clean up. Walt Garrison was already in there, and soon after, Lee Roy came in. Walt said to him, "Lee Roy, I sure hate you're going to sit out against Kansas City. We could beat the hell out of them if you stayed in." Well, I didn't know what that meant exactly. Walt was a redneck white boy who could talk crazy and would say anything he felt like saying. Sometimes he could be a funny guy, so maybe he was just razzing me, but maybe he really thought I couldn't handle the middle. Most of the guys agreed that I could play a little bit, but the question was, could I go the extra mile necessary to play the middle? So Walt's words kind of stirred me up inside. He'd pretty much said that I couldn't play all that well.

I don't think he had that same attitude after the game with the Chiefs. I put Ed Podolak out of the game. I put Warren McVea out of the game. I was tearing them up. When I hit, I wasn't playing. I was trying to knock them out. Then I played against center Jack Rudnay. He was a Super Bowl champ and a multiple-time All-Pro and Pro Bowler, but he didn't have a chance because I was too quick. You had to be a quick, knowledgeable center to stop me. There were a few of those, like Mike Webster with the Pittsburgh Steelers, who was considered to be one of the best centers in NFL history. Webster was the same height as me but was thirty or more pounds heavier. I'd never seen a center that good. He didn't fool around and could tear you up. There was no contest if he got to me, so I really had to get into position against him and bob and weave or get a little lower to defeat him. Plus the rest of my guys had to play just right because Pittsburgh had a dynamite offensive line. Unfortunately, we lost that game.

Soon after we played the Chiefs, we were in a meeting, and one of the coaches said,

"Rodrigo Barnes graded out at 10+." That means I scored 10 points higher than anticipated. Well, everybody—the veterans included—turned around and looked at me and said, "Wow!"

DD said, "Man, you tore 'em up!" No other Cowboy had ever graded out like that under Landry. It was unheard of, but I didn't know that. I didn't even know what it meant, and Landry didn't ever tell you anything—and neither did the other coaches or the players. The team was screwed up in that respect, and Landry was always playing psychological games.

Thanks in part to me, the Cowboys' prospects were looking up, but that didn't mean an improvement to my condition. Lee Roy, of course, didn't like me too much because he could see I was a threat to his position, and he didn't want me to play at all. And because he was a star, the coaches didn't like me either and warned me that I was coming on too strong. "You're just a rookie," they said. That's the way it was in the pros. Sometimes it seemed as if you had to fight your own team before you battled the enemy.

Lee Roy came back after that to start against the Miami Dolphins in our final preseason game. I was given the weak-side linebacker position, but not as a starter. Even here, though, I more than proved my worth when I played. I stopped fullback Larry Csonka three times in the hole number one, which is right beside the center. Nobody had ever done that before. And I was 6'1" and 225 pounds. It wasn't like I was 250. But I had leverage, and I knew how to hit and tackle. I also knew to approach Csonka early, before he'd churned up and was rolling downhill on me. I caught him before he even got past the scrimmage line, before he got up a full head of steam. For me to catch him and stop him point blank, well, they'd never seen that before. And I did it on the goal line.

Stopping Csonka was really something, and the coaches were hollering and screaming, and the announcer was saying, "Did you see that Rodrigo Barnes?" and all that sort of stuff. So I was rolling good, but none of that seemed to affect Landry. After that, I found myself just standing on the sidelines because he wouldn't let me have a place. Even though he saw that I was playing really well, for some reason, he wouldn't give me a shot at the position I wanted. He'd practice me in one position but play me in another during the game. And he wouldn't give me an explanation but just said nothing. I thought, *Darn, they don't even want to give me a chance to compete.* After the Miami game, as we were getting ready to begin the regular season, those of us who survived the final cut left the Ramada Inn to settle into our own homes. But that didn't mean I was settled in with the Cowboys. I'd seen an opening right in front of me because of those first two games, but Landry closed it up tight. Maybe that was partly my fault, because around this time, I made another tremendous mistake regarding Landry. A reporter came to me and said, "I hear you're afraid of Coach Landry."

And me being me and nave, too, I replied, "I'm just as afraid of Coach Landry as he is of me." That statement probably erased any possibility that Landry might start me in the middle.

Landry still wasn't talking to me personally about playing the middle. Instead, he sent his guys—managers, coaches, and so forth—to tell me that starting in the middle wasn't going to happen for me. They offered me starting outside linebacker instead, but I turned it down, saying no, I wanted to play the middle. I knew that my skills and abilities were best in the middle. They came to me a total of three times, and my answer was the same each time: "No, I want to play the middle." I must be the only player in the Cowboys' history to turn down a starting position, and it was the worst mistake of my life because it not only guaranteed that I wouldn't start, but it also virtually relegated me to special teams where it's easy to get hurt.

What I really needed was for Landry to come to me himself to explain why he was doing things that way instead of sending others to do it for him. If he'd just told me, "I want to start you as outside linebacker, and I'll look at you later on for the middle. But right now, we're a team, and I need you to play this position for the team. That's how you can help." I wasn't the type player who wouldn't do what the head coach told me to do, but I needed to hear it from his own mouth, not through the words of others. One good conversation with the king would have resolved all those issues for me. But Landry and I didn't communicate. I think now that he might have sent his guys instead of coming himself to protect me from myself—from doing or saying something stupid that would rile him up enough to get rid of me.

But that one good conversation with Landry never happened, and I was egotistical and naive enough that I kept thinking that Landry was going to release the defense to me and I'd get another opportunity to play middle linebacker, but that's not how things transpired. The competition was over with, and that was that. Some opportunities knock only once, and if you want them, you'd better grab them, because after that, they evaporate. I can see now that my ego messed me up. I thought that everything was about me, and I couldn't see that my own attitude only served to defeat me.

After my refusal, Landry started D. D. Lewis as outside linebacker. Although DD had been around for four or five years, he'd never started. He been playing behind Chuck Howley, and nobody was going to beat out Chuck, who was a great player. But at the moment, there wasn't much time to ponder my situation because the regular season—my first pro season—was about to begin.

CHAPTER
10

PLAYING FOR THE COWBOYS—SEASON ONE

The Cowboys played well during my first season with them, and we almost went to the Super Bowl. My friend DD had a good year, and so did a lot of the other guys.

Our first game was against the Chicago Bears at Soldier Field. In one play, Bob Newhouse charged in to block Dick Butkus. There have been a lot of great middle linebackers since those days, but back then, Butkus was considered the best to have played the game. And when Newhouse charged in there, Butkus caught him just right and sent him flying backward. It was like watching a BB bounce off a steel wall and pretty funny to see. You can be sure that Newhouse didn't try that again against Butkus.

Mostly it was hard work, but we had our fun, too, and we always had these little challenges going on. One funny incident started in the locker room after our second or third game, while the defense was suiting up for practice. Several of us began arguing over who was fastest, and Calvin Hill piped up and told me, "I can beat you in the 40." The 40-yard dash is the standard distance in the NFL for players, like linebackers and defensive backs, who have to do a lot of running. Personally, I think 40 isn't enough, and it should be increased to 60.

Anyway, when Calvin said that, naturally I responded, "Naw, you can't beat me in the

40." At the same time, Bob Hayes and Golden Richards also were arguing about which of them was fastest. Golden was quick, but Bob, you'll remember, was considered the fastest human on the planet. He was, however, thirty-one, and maybe Golden thought age had slowed him down. By now, there was nothing else to do but go out on the field to settle the matter with a 40-yard dash between the two pairs of challengers: Bob Hayes versus Golden Richards and Calvin Hill versus me. First it was Calvin and me. We lined up, and when the guy calling the race shouted, "Go!" I was gone. I stayed low and kept my form and crossed the finish line way ahead of my opponent, thinking, *Eat my dust, Calvin Hill.* The truth is, though, that while I might have been able to beat Calvin in flat-out racing, he could outrun me on offensive patterns. The funniest part is that, to this day, Calvin wants a rematch.

Then it was time for Golden and Bob to race, and Bob said, "I'll give you a three-yard lead and still beat you." Golden didn't say anything to that, but you could see that he was thinking, *Shoot, if you give me three yards, I'll beat you for sure.* They lined up, the starter called, "Go," and they went. At about twenty-five yards, Bob started walking on Golden, at thirty he was even, and by the time he reached the 40, he was a full yard ahead. I think that Golden was disappointed. He was a fast cat, and he didn't think Bob could take him in the 40, especially with a three-yard lead.

But Bullet Bob always was an impressive runner, and he knew it. About this time, he made it known that he wanted more money—I guess he was making seventy to eighty thousand a year—but the Cowboys weren't going to give it to him. Joe Namath said that if Bob came up to New York, he'd give Bob $10,000 of his own money, but Bob didn't take him up on that. In 1975, though, he was traded to the San Francisco 49ers for third-round draft choice Duke Fergerson.

But while Bob was with the Cowboys, he was worth every penny of his salary. He changed football. Bob made NFL teams abandon man-to-man cover, which used to be the norm. Because he could beat everybody, opposing teams had to start using zone coverage, also known as zone defense, which is used to cover particular areas of the playing field to make it difficult for quarterbacks to pass effectively. The same sort of thing happened in the NBA when it went to mostly black players since some of those white boys couldn't cover the black players man-to-man. It's hard to cover any great player man-to-man anyway. Take Larry Byrd. You can't cover him man-to-man.

So the NFL had to change the rules and tactics to keep certain players playing and maintain their identities as the greatest players in the world who could do things nobody else could. That might have kept the crowds coming, but it also shut out other players who, as a result, weren't allowed to participate and show their stuff. And I believed I was one of those left out. What I wanted from the Cowboys was to be the middle linebacker. That's the guy who runs the show and makes it happen. But they didn't want me in that position even though I'd done really well in the preseason.

Middle linebacker was one of the breakthrough positions in the league for black players, and at the time, the league wasn't eager for any black players to do any breaking through. In fact, there wasn't any sort of push for black heroes in any sport, except maybe track and field, where competition tends to be between individuals rather than teams. So black athletes were not going to be running the show for any team—either as quarterbacks or middle linebackers. Before their merger with the NFL, the AFL allowed black players in all positions, so when the leagues joined, there were some black players in those positions. But when I was playing for the Cowboys, there were only two black middle linebacker in the NFL: me and Hall of Famer Willie Lanier, who played for the Kansas City Chiefs.

Whatever the ultimate reason—Landry, league politics, racial bias, or my own stubbornness—I wasn't allowed to start during the season. But that didn't deter me. I played hard and kicked butt. I was good, and everybody knew it. As the season went on, it was hard not to recognize that Lee Roy didn't want to have too much to do with me because he knew I was coming up and at him. If you read the newspaper articles published at the time, I was the talk of the town because I was bagging it up. I had great instincts, and I could read my opponents pretty well.

But the one person I didn't read well was the guy upstairs. You have to read the guy upstairs as much as you do the opposition. While you're out there making plays, the guy upstairs is watching your every move, observing your tendencies, and figuring you out so he can use you to the best advantage based on how you react in certain situations. Discovering that was all a part of playing, learning, and being engaged.

As time went on, I learned more and more, but I hadn't gotten to the point of figuring out Landry, other than not to anger him in front of anybody. Unfortunately, my ego and pride had taken me over. All the time I was making plays and hearing the crowds cheer, I was thinking it was all about me and that I was great—that I was the one making everything happen. I totally forgot who I was and how I'd gotten to where I was—how many people had helped me along the way and how much my teammates contributed to my successes. That's how deeply immersed I was in my own ego.

The part that made it really bad was that I thought I was okay. I hadn't yet learned that achievement, success, and position aren't truly real if you think you're okay when you're not. And I was messing up all the time without realizing it. Landry had offered me a starting linebacker job, but because it wasn't the middle, I refused it. I got so caught up in my ego that I forgot what I was there for. I just couldn't think or see the truth about myself.

But it seemed that fighting against almost everybody and everything had become a way of life. Maybe that was partly because of all the fighting I'd done to rise out of the projects and to address social injustices almost everywhere I went. Whatever the cause, it seemed that my "fighting valve" was open wide, and I was caught up in a pattern of conflict for the sake of conflict. When you get like that—like I was—you get to the point where you forget what you're there for. I was there to play football, but I found myself immersed in personal battles for sake of the battle rather than to see an outcome. And those kinds of ego issues extended into all parts of my life. Instead of playing in a way that made the whole team viable, I was focusing my energy and expectations on making big plays that would make me stand out.

Because I couldn't see the truth about myself, I started blaming other people for my faults and lack of advancement—especially Landry. I was angry that he wouldn't let me start in the middle, and I totally ignored the fact that he offered to let me start on the outside. If I'd really looked at the situation, I would have seen that, as the coach, he was in the best position to know what was right for the team and that he was giving me a really great opportunity. Starting on the outside wasn't starting in the middle, but it was starting nonetheless. Essentially he was giving me almost everything I wanted, so what was my problem?

Me. I was the real problem. My behavior was weird, but when you're egotistical, you can't see yourself. The truth is, it's very hard to criticize and change oneself. To do that, you have to stay on point all the time. You can't go to sleep. You can't be sitting around thinking about something else. You have to take care of business and pay attention to your job. You can take a break every once in a while, but you can't be tripping and stuff because, before you know it, you're out of focus, you're not seeing right, you're not hearing right, and your understanding is wrong.

Taking Stock

Everything was going in my favor, then suddenly, it wasn't. I was an inch shy here, or a step short there. I thought that success would be just a matter of having an opportunity to do what I wanted, but I was learning that wasn't necessarily the case. The one thing I did have besides my skills and abilities was that the fans were behind me and wanted to know what was going on and why I wasn't playing more. But if there were issues with a player, the Cowboys were always going to lay the blame on the player and deny that the coaches had anything to do with it.

And the stresses on the players were compounded by internal team regulations that did nothing to help them. If you got hurt, you didn't go to the training room or get in the whirlpool or anything like that. It was weird. Even though you were there, your position was tenuous. It wasn't like it had been in college, where everybody on the team was tight. The pros are a business, and the culture was very divisive even though we were supposed to be working together as a team. But the only time we were together was on game day. Then, we were 100 percent for each other, but it was different during practice and other times, such as meetings.

At this one meeting, for example, we discussed a perennial problem we seemed to have when the opposition kicker kicked the ball into one of the two corners. I was on the front line of the kickoff receive team, and those of us on the line were watching the opposition, so we couldn't turn around to see if the ball's trajectory went straight or curved after it passed over us. We might be in a right-return pattern, but if the ball was kicked to the left corner, the opposition would tear right through us. Landry said we should be able to track the ball, and I piped up and said, "We can't see the ball once it's behind us, Coach. When it goes over our heads, it looks like it's going straight. We can't tell if it curves toward a corner after that. All we can do is watch where the opposition goes after the kick."

After I said that, you could hear a pin drop. People just didn't say things like that to Landry—especially a black player and a rookie to boot. I was just trying to help the team, but when I'd do stuff like that, the other guys would look at me like they were scared or I was nuts for bucking Landry since he'd cut players for speaking out like that.

Worse, sometimes the other coaches would tell you to do something, and you'd do it only to discover that Landry didn't like it. When he asked you why you did it at the next meeting, the coaches wouldn't admit to him they'd told you to do it because they were too scared. That left you to shoulder the blame and fear reprimand. But the problem with all that created fear is that fear, no matter where it comes from, will defeat you. When you have fear, you have a lack of communication, a lack of reality, and a lack of drive.

I noticed that, and I was a little disappointed, especially when I saw that praise was light and criticism and punishment were heavy and unequally distributed. Some players could screw up, and Landry wouldn't say a thing about it, while others would get ridden by him in the meetings for almost nothing. In fact, the whole situation grew strange. I had my own opinions and thoughts, and those didn't always align with the coaches' ideas of who I was and what I could do. I wasn't preaching my philosophy to my teammates, but just the fact that I did have opinions and expressed them was a problem. And the opinions of any player that didn't coincide with those of the coaches usually made it upstairs, one way or another. On every team there are players who run to management to tell tales out of school. I guess every organization, sports or otherwise, has someone like that.

I don't know if Landry remained distant because of what he was being told about me. It was difficult to communicate with him and arrive at some kind of understanding. But while his behavior intimidated most of the other players, it didn't intimidate me. You could be a giant, and I wouldn't be intimidated because fear takes away your spirit. I wasn't about to go around with my head hung down, and the team certainly wasn't paying me enough for me to violate my personality or principles.

As far as my teammates went, a lot of them didn't know how to deal with me because I wasn't an Uncle Tom doing whatever management dictated. The truth was, they didn't understand what I was doing because they were all looking the other way, scared. Even the so-called stars were scared. I was amazed at that. Now, Bob Hayes was different. He was free in spirit, and he didn't get into that cycle of fear. He was Bullet Bob, laughing and joking and enjoying life while most of the rest of the players were uptight. There were one or two trying to emulate Bob, but none of them had the kind of history he did to back them up.

Mel Renfro, who was normally a quiet guy, said to me one day, "I'm scared for you, man. If you keep saying things, they're going to get rid of you." He'd seen it happen to a lot of players. Even *I'd* seen it happen. But I didn't know any way to be other than the way I was. I wasn't trying to be insolent, but I was in a macho, man's sport, and although there were a lot of things I needed to learn and needed help with, those didn't include learning to be intimidated. Being intimidated would weaken me, and I wasn't about to let that happen. But it seemed that I was alone in this, and I was amazed to see black star players walking around in fear, unable to enjoy themselves or even understand who they were.

I didn't get it, but that's the way the situation was, and that's the way the players were. But I was willing to sacrifice management's pride of control and the players' fear to maintain my personal freedom. Freedom was important to me because I'd gown up in the Jim Crow era, and I saw and experienced that stuff that you read about in the earlier chapters on my childhood. When I got free of the subservient mindset I'd been immersed in back in Waco, I determined that I wasn't going to give up my freedom for anyone or anything—not even to start for the Cowboys.

Freedom of expression was part of that. I realized that I'd have to suffer for my candor and that some people didn't like it and didn't like me for it. And truthfully, some of them didn't even like me being who I was. I wasn't tall, light brown, and pretty haired. I was the real-deal brother with dark skin and a big nose. But even though I didn't win all the time, I felt pretty secure being me and wasn't about to be deterred from my beliefs because being real was the only thing I wanted. But society wasn't ready for that from African Americans.

Especially in Dallas. A good example is Bill Thomas, who'd been drafted the year before me and played second team. Thomas was from Boston College, and he met this white chick he ended up marrying. Now I don't know much about Boston, but I later lived there long enough to learn that it was a little like Mississippi in terms of race. The Cowboys had a venue for entertainment attached to their practice facility, and Bill and his girl got married there, and the coaches and management weren't prepared for that, although they smiled and pretended they were. But at the end of that season, they got rid of Bill. They didn't want a black player walking around Dallas with a white wife or for him to become a star and his interracial marriage to become more obvious.

No one should be surprised, though. As I said earlier, in terms of cities, Dallas was a prime redneck capital of the South. Frequently when I drove around, I'd be stopped by the police, pulled over about nothing. They intimidated, threatened, and talked bad to me. That sort of thing went on in Dallas until the mid-1990s, when it started slowing down, but back then, they'd shoot and kill you. It was a little like the situation today in some cities, only worse. I guess some of those police just couldn't be happy unless they killed somebody black. I'd played so well early in the season that I thought I was right at the crest of making it big as a middle linebacker. Surely something would happen later on, and I'd get to start. But while I did manage to play a few games—third downs and passing downs and stuff—and did well on the special teams, I didn't get to start. I promised myself that next year I was going to take Lee Roy's job or somebody's job and start. I was headstrong and a little angry at Landry, too, for not letting me play more, but in the end, I understood. Lee Roy was a veteran and a great player, and while he might once have been better than he now was, he still was no slouch. His game was going, and he went to the Pro Bowl and helped propel the Cowboys to the playoffs. We didn't quite make the Super Bowl, though, losing the NFC championship game against Minnesota. I was really disappointed that we didn't make it because that year the

Super Bowl was played in Rice Stadium, and I really wanted to play that game there.

But even if we'd won the championship against Minnesota, I might not have played in the Super Bowl because during the game, I injured my left knee. That news was bad enough, but then the doctors told me that although I'd passed several physicals when I joined the Cowboys, apparently they hadn't thoroughly checked my right knee—the one I'd hurt during my last year at Rice. Now they noticed that the older injury was worse than the newer one, and I had to face the fact that both my knees were messed up.

I went to Houston for the surgery, and the doctors operated on the older injury first, with the surgery on my other knee planned for the following year. After the operation, I stayed in Houston to recuperate. I also worked out, trying to keep in shape for the next season and trying to get my head back together. I was frustrated that I'd messed up, especially since I knew that if I'd been starting and hadn't been playing so much for the special teams, I wouldn't have gotten hurt. Things weren't going right, and there were bad feelings all the way around, largely because of the way I was looking at things through my ego and reacting to them through my pride. Like I said, I was pretty messed up in the head, and with both knees injured, my prospects were dimming. I knew I'd have to take a whole new approach to both football and life.

So I spent the summer pondering on where I was and what was going on. Things that year had started out fine, but the season, already tumultuous enough, had ended on a sour note. I was still a Dallas Cowboy, but my situation was precarious. Everything that I thought and hoped was going to happen hadn't—none of it. Worse, with two bad knees, my stock went down in the eyes of the Cowboy organization. After only one year of pro football, it seemed that my game was pretty much over.

CHAPTER 11

PLAYING FOR THE COWBOYS—SEASON TWO

I was a day late returning to training camp my second season with the Cowboys because I had to get a doctor's approval to show I was ready to play. I didn't think too much of being a day late, but the Cowboys organization was a little upset with me about that. On the first week I was still recuperating from my knee surgery, so the coaches took it easy on me and kept my contact work low. As far as they were concerned, there was no pressure for me to perform at a high level since they weren't looking to start me, and from my own standpoint, I wasn't competing for a starting position that year anyway. I was just trying to get back in shape to play.

In the beginning, I was working out three-a-days with Otto Stowe and another guy. The coaches had me doing it to get back in shape, but Otto was out there because he wouldn't work out on the weights. We'd get up about 6:00 a.m., and the coaches would run us on 120-yard strides. We started out running ten stretches in a row, and between each, we'd walk for something like ten seconds. Over the span of just a few days, we worked up to fifteen stretches. After the coaches ran us for forty-five minutes or so, they made us do a few agility workouts. It was all good conditioning, and I didn't mind.

That year, our defense shifted around a little bit. Bob Lilly was still hanging on, Jethro Pugh was still there, and Billy Joe DuPree was doing fine. Harvey Martin was coming on and beginning to play more as right defensive end. D. D. Lewis took over weak-side linebacker duties from Chuck Howley, who retired. DD was a small guy for the pros, but he performed well on the weak side for nine seasons. Ed "Too Tall" Jones came in and took left defensive end. Too Tall was the first pick in the 1974 draft, and when you're the number one pick, you're definitely going to be a starter. Plus, because he was a first-round pick, the team was obliged to pay him more. In fact, he was the first black player who came into the Cowboys making any real money, and the rest of us black players were proud of him for that. He proved to be a good player and a good guy. At first, he split time with Pat Toomay, who was a solid player, but at the end of the season, the team let Toomay's option run out, and he ended up going to the Buffalo Bills.

Strike

The team itself seemed to be in good shape as the preseason approached, but Gil Brandt and Tex Schramm, who was the Cowboys' original president and general manager, were handling some issues. The main one was that the players wanted more money, and the Cowboys didn't want to give it to them unless, as with Too Tall, they were forced to. We were in one meeting where Landry said, "You guys don't need any money unless you're just broke." I thought that was a ridiculous statement, in and of itself, and showed that he was totally insensitive to people's needs, aspirations, family situations, and so forth. I guess he was blunt like that because he wanted to exert some control over the situation, which wasn't isolated to the Cowboys. There was unrest throughout the league over pay, and the National Football League Players Association intended to mount a strike.

The NFLPA, of which I was a member, had been in existence only since 1970, but it had already struck once on behalf of the players. That had been under founding president and former player John Mackey, who'd been advised by attorney Ed Garvey. Mackey stepped down in 1973, and after Garvey took the reins of the organization, he tried to motivate the players to strike for better conditions as well as for higher pay. We did go on strike right at the beginning of the 1974 season, and the strife it caused made for a hard year and created a lot of divisions within the team and between some of the players.

When there's a strike during preseason, none of the players go to camp, and that, of course, led to one of the most direct issues affecting players during the strike: dwindling paychecks. If we weren't practicing and playing, the owners weren't paying. That spelled tough economic times, especially for those of us players at the lower end of the pay scale. Eventually, I found out that the Players Association had hardship money to distribute to different guys during the strike, though it took some time for me to learn about that. I think it was Jean Fugett, who was a tight end behind DuPree at the time, who was our team's representative to the NFLPA. Being one of the lower-paid players, I went to him to ask for some financial help, but he acted as if he didn't know anything about the relief funds and wouldn't give me a cent. I was disappointed, but there wasn't anything I could do about it.

As the strike loomed then progressed, the owners tried everything they could to exert control, including replacing or even destroying players who were disruptive. But they discovered that the public didn't buy it, and they had to come to the bargaining table. As we'd pointed out to them time and time again, they might have thought they were the stars, but without the players, there is no game and there is no NFL.

The Players Association and the owners finally met. That was in Chicago, and I attended as an alternate representative for the Cowboys. That was the first time I'd ever been involved in anything like that or had the chance to listen directly to the owners to see how they viewed players. What I learned in that meeting was disappointing. The owners clearly looked at players the same way a stable owner looks at racehorses—not as individuals but as products to be exploited. They didn't have much respect, or anything else, for the players and didn't really understand that the fans don't come to see the owners sitting in the stands but to watch the players compete on the gridiron.

It's a ridiculous situation that continues today. Jerry Jones, the current owner of the Cowboys, is a case in point. I like Jones for being the first owner of the franchise to really pay players other than the quarterbacks: the wide receivers and the other playmakers. Those are the guys putting their bodies and well-being on the line, and Jones gave them a chance to earn some real money for it. But I don't like the way he does the players. His philosophy is, "Don't let the inmates run the prison." For players, that's kind of an insult because in any pro sport, the players are equal to or greater in importance than the owners.

So when we finally sat down at the bargaining table, I saw that the owners had no concern or respect for the players, but I also saw that the players themselves didn't realize that they'd been the true victors and were the ones who actually controlled the league. I blame the Players Association leadership for downplaying that vital aspect. That was the one megaweapon the players possessed when facing down the big guns brought by the owners—and the owners had some really big guns. But the players never deployed that megaweapon. Instead, they just let the owners open with a barrage from their own arsenal. The owners' strategy was to hammer and break us. I guess that's what people in that position do. They want to break you psychologically and economically and make you subservient to them.

First came the media blitz. The owners had most, though not all, of the press in their pockets—more so than now. Reporters all over were kissing the owners' butts so they could get paid to travel to games, stay in fancy hotels, and get special seating for their families and friends as well as tips and insider information. That meant that reporters were committed to supporting the owners' desires and points of view, and they did that through articles and sportscasts, often making the players look as if we were striking for selfish and greedy reasons.

It didn't seem to matter that none of that was true, and a lot of those reporters knew better. You might remember that I met Tommy Jackson in the Blue–Gray game. After his playing days were over, Tommy went on to become an announcer for ESPN, where he ended up working for nearly thirty years. He was an expert and an insider, and he should have understood what was really going on, but he made statements he had to have known weren't right or true. I guess he'd say those things because he was caught up in the situation and his position instead of stepping back, examining matters, and saying something real.

One of the owners' most important weapons was the Willie Lynch process of using fear and intimidation to turn the oppressed against each other. The owners, through management and coaches, would terrorize and punish those who didn't accept subservience, and players who balked would be demeaned—and sometimes vilified—in the press. The tenseness of the situation incited and reinforced the fear of that happening, pressuring everyone to support the system. Even the players' family members were not immune because they'd want to help their loved ones and see them succeed instead of being in pain from mistreatment.

Willie Lynch was so powerful that it could be used to incite and promote fear and subservience through generations of players. When you came in as a rookie, the more experienced players would tell you, "Hey, man, you better watch this, and you better not do that," and so forth. It was just like what went on with the kneeling situation in the NFL, with Jerry Jones, and even the president of the country calling the kneeling players "sons of bitches" and other derogatory terms. Basically, the owners will use any means at their disposal—even if it isn't true or valid—to maintain control over every aspect of the lives of the players under them. Once you introduce that kind of fear into an organization, the players themselves will institutionalize and spread it to other players. It's brainwashing, and like an infection, it even contaminates college players.

In addition to being bolstered by external factors, like the press, Willie Lynch was further cemented into place by inner urges to reap the rewards of capitulation. The egos and pride of the players, who often wanted to be big shots not only on the field but also in the newspapers so they could be famous or find financial reward, took over. That made the players even more complicit in perpetuating the system that held them in thrall, and all the while, the owners just lay back, took the money, and used these tools to control and manipulate the players. It's a shame that the players' loyalty and lack of experience and maturity were exploited like that. Instead of being conscious of what was really going on, they simply buried their heads in the sand.

For a lot of players, that continues after retirement. They miss the limelight and being around all that excitement and everything that goes along with it, and they'll do anything to stay in it. I've seen some great players—All-Pros and others—running around, kissing the owner's butt just to hang around. So the owners use free tickets to get players to make appearances at games, and in return, the players are supposed to go around and glad-hand with all the boosters in the private suites.

And the players oblige instead of saying, "This isn't football. This is economic and political power tripping designed to keep the players in line and under control." But too few players dared stand up to the many pressures and complain about the situation. Instead, they continue to do the Willie Lynch thing to new generations of players, pretending that pro football is the greatest thing in the world and that life out in the real world doesn't count. Watching all that going on in pro ball changed me because I just couldn't get behind that sort of thinking and behavior. It was opposite to my nature. I'd grown up under Jim Crow and Willie Lynch, without position, privilege, or promise, so it was easy to see exactly how the owners maintained control over the players. And worse was how the players' representatives reacted and took advantage of the players, too, almost setting them up for failure.

For one thing, the Players Association called the strike at the beginning of the season, which is a pattern they still follow. But if there's going to be a strike, that's the time that the owners and league official prefer because they hold all the financial cards Striking at the beginning of the season means that players won't get paid at the end of the off-season—the very time they are at their most financially vulnerable. And really, who cares about a strike during preseason? The owners and NFL officials try to make the players and the public believe that training camp is important, but it's not. That time is mostly filled with practice and preseason games that don't count, and all the players get out of it is little bitty money.

All too often, the players acted as if they couldn't understand the issues themselves. They seemed to take no interest in or control over their own futures and were content to let somebody else tell them who should be the leader of the Players Association and what its policies should be. If I'd been the leader of the association, I'd have called the strike during the playoffs, when the players held real leverage over the owners. If a striking team doesn't play, there are no stadium sellouts and no TV revenues, and the team can't possibly be a Super Bowl winner. And as for the players, they would have received most of their season's pay to keep them going financially and, in the end, retained a little dignity and self-respect. Playing and winning games will always come later. You don't have to worry about that. America loves football, and it's not going to stop watching it.

But the representatives for the Players Association would sell out the players in favor of the owners, and then the owners accomplished the coup de grâce with the quarterbacks, whom they used to control the team. You'd think that the quarterbacks would care about their linemen and receivers, but every time the players struck, the quarterbacks would sell them out by running straight into camp, saying, "I'm not going to sit out and not get paid." And because the strike was called at the beginning of the season when the players needed their paychecks most, the rest of them ended up dragging back into camp like sheep, looking foolish for having tried to stand up for their rights. I'm not going to call the players stupid—but most were extremely naive and will go for the ruse every time. They'll let the quarterbacks lead them even if the quarterbacks don't care anything about them. It's happened time and time again, and watching it, I'm just flabbergasted.

There is another endemic problem with the league that the Players Association also lets slide. Too often, teams pay a premium for some players while asking other players to take pay cuts. I'll use the example of Aaron Rogers. He wanted $35 million, which left the Green Bay Packers without enough money for their other players. Now, I'm not blaming Aaron Rogers for that. He's entitled to ask for what he thinks he's worth, but the situation highlights one simple fact: It's not the responsibility of players to use their own money to pay other players. It's the responsibility of the owners to pay everyone.

Some players buy into that mindset and take pay cuts, but taking a cut doesn't always have the desired results, especially when you have the hardness and narrowness of an organization like the New England Patriots, whom I later played for. Tom Brady took a cut so that the Patriots could pay some of the other guys, but when it came time for Randy Moss to get paid, they didn't pay him. They cut him. Then Moss came back with, "I love New England." Wow. How Willie Lynch can you be if you can do something like that? Now, I respected Moss as a player. I think he was probably the best wide receiver in the league in his day for his ability to catch long passes. But when it came to stuff like loyalty, well, some people hold higher regard for those who deal the deal instead of to the ideas of teamwork or loyalty to fellow players. They can't buck the Willie Lynch mindset, so they just stick with it, no matter how undignified that is.

Finally, Ed Garvey announced that the strike was over and that we had a deal. But the deal wasn't anything. The strike proved to be a farce, and the players got nothing for it—no money, no nothing. It was totally ridiculous. Garvey, and most of the guys who represented us in the Players Association sold us out. And the situation remains pretty much the same today. The NFLPA is still mounting strikes at the beginning of the season, saying, "We're shutting down training camp," and acting like that's a big deal.

On top of that, the NFLPA eventually made an agreement that any decision the commissioner makes regarding players or problems is the final word. That means that now there is no appeal process for players who dispute the commissioner's decision. And those decisions can punish a player for actions in his personal life that are not illegal and have nothing to do with football but that might incense the public. Many such matters should be left to the player's team to resolve, but now the commissioner can come in and make a ruling, and the players can't appeal. I just can't understand why the NFLPA would give away its power to the commissioner and make him god over the league. That's essentially giving the owners total control over the players.

And not only had we been sold out, but we also were treated even worse than before *because* we'd struck. If you were one of the big shots on the team, well, no problem. But if you were anybody else, you were fixing to catch hell, and I happened to be one of those other guys fixing to catch hell. Worse, they wanted someone to blame everything on, somebody to be the scapegoat, and who better than me? Rodrigo Barnes was the person they blamed. It almost was like déjà vu. I'd been good on the field for the Rice Owls, but when I shook the university's tree by picketing for better representation of minorities on campus, they turned against me. And now the Cowboys were doing the same thing.

I realized that there wasn't much I could do about the situation. The Cowboys' powers that be would do what they wanted to do, and if that meant I wouldn't get the chance to do what I wanted with them, well, I wasn't dead or incapacitated. I could get by. I'd never lived all that high on the hog, anyway, and I knew that I could survive at my current economic level or do even better by working some regular job.

Anything would be better than having my mind twisted like the owners and the Players Association tried to do to us.

Back in Play

After the strike and in the middle of all the fallout from it, we started playing. I'd recuperated by the end of camp and was bouncing around between several positions—second-team middle linebacker behind Lee Roy Jordan, weak-side linebacker, and strong safety—as well as playing on special teams. After we broke camp, we flew to New Orleans to play the Saints in our first preseason game before going back to Dallas. Usually we flew to games in nice planes, but on this occasion, we had to ride in a twin-engine propeller plane. On top of that, the weather was bad, so it was an unusual trip to say the least. The game was played in Tulane Stadium since the Louisiana Superdome—now called the Mercedes-Benz Superdome—had yet to be built. We were confident going into the game, but New Orleans jumped all over us. For a while, we thought we might be able to get up on them or even beat them, but that didn't happen.

By game five, we were 1–4, and right after that, Landry called me into his office. I walked in and sat down, and he said, "We're going to have to let you go, Rodrigo." There was no explanation, though he did mention my bad knees.

I said, "Okay, Coach." What else could I say? I got up, shook his hand, and walked out. I went on back to my apartment, thinking I'd have to find something else to do besides play football. I sat around for four weeks, but all that time, even though Landry had effectively fired me, the Cowboys kept me on the string and wouldn't officially cut me. That meant I couldn't play, and they wouldn't pay me either, leaving me stuck in a bad situation professionally and economically.

While I was out, the Cowboys started winning again, but that didn't do anything for me since I still wasn't getting any money, nor would they release me, which also meant I couldn't go to another team. All I could do, day after day, was just sit there in my high-rise apartment, staring through the windows, mulling over my situation, and trying to figure out where I might go and what I might do once I was released— if I was released, which didn't seem likely any time soon. All the while, the Cowboys' coaches and management were trying to decide how to deal with me because they had to do it in a very public way. And they weren't about to let me off lightly. They wanted to make me the villain of the story and to come out of this thing a winner.

They did that using their two reliable tools: the press and Willie Lynch. News about the situation leaked out to the media, but instead of reporting accurately, the press twisted the story. Like I said, the reporters were in the owners' pockets, and most of them were happy to go along when the Cowboys started making me a political target, saying that I was trying to be a clubhouse lawyer and control the team. The team's management made it seem that I deliberately wasn't coming to practice, and the newspaper guys supported that story even though everybody knew better. Pretty soon, the fans were repeating what the press was putting out: Rodrigo Barnes is a smart-ass troublemaker and has gone and quit on the Cowboys.

My teammates said nothing because they were too scared to speak out. Anybody associated with me was in jeopardy. After a while, whenever I went to a new team, my reputation followed, and the owners and press made my reputation the deal rather than my playing. The paranoia was just rampant thanks. In many ways, pro athletes are the most cowardly guys when it comes to standing up for themselves because they're into that fame and money game, and they're afraid they might lose both. They don't have any dignity. In pro sports, the notions of "team" and "teammates" mean nothing. You could be best friends today, but if you're cut, you're out of the picture. For them, loyalty is nothing beyond a talking point. Their loyalty lies solely with the ownership and their paycheck, and to please the former and keep the latter, they'll sell out anybody.

I couldn't let this no-play-and-no-pay situation go on indefinitely. After four weeks, I was out of money, forcing me to go to the NFL Council for assistance. After all, what the Cowboys were doing to me was in violation not only of NFL rules but also of federal labor laws. I explained the situation to the council and asked them to help me to get paid and get released so I could try to find another team to hire me. Trying to be as fair as possible, I even told the NFL that although Landry said he wanted to get rid of me, I didn't think he really meant it. He just didn't know how to handle the situation. I guess I was young and naive and trying to understand the situation and see the best. But the truth is, I liked playing for the Cowboys, and I liked my teammates. I didn't have a problem with any of that. It was the team—or probably more accurately, Tex Schramm—who had a problem with me.

Abner Haynes, an all-time great player who, along with Leon King, integrated Texas college football in 1957, went to Landry as my representative.

"It doesn't make sense to cut Rodrigo like this," he told Landry, then he proposed that I could get operated on that year and sit out the rest of the season. After that, Landry could decide what to do with me. But I'd have to get paid while I was out so that I could afford the operation and to cover my living expenses until I could play again.

I might have had my own immature moments with Landry, but now that it was time for him to put on the big-boy shirt, he didn't. He and Schramm were hot because I'd brought the NFL Council in to put pressure on them to give me my money, and they were done with me. Landry told Abner that he wouldn't let me come back, and my need for another surgery merely legitimized his cutting me.

And with that, it was all over between the Dallas Cowboys and me. In the end, the NFL forced the Cowboys to send me my back pay, and I left the team with six games to go in the season.

Part Four
The Bouncing Football

CHAPTER

12

THE NEW ENGLAND PATRIOTS

A football can bounce in crazy directions, and the same goes for football players. Once the Cowboys released me, the NFL again had me in their sights, and they sent me to the New England Patriots. It wasn't that the Patriots picked me up. Instead, the NFL just sent me there. I had no choice in the matter except to quit playing football. It was kind of like an undercover trade deal with the Cowboys. In the NFL, there were all these little hooks. Players didn't know the details, but even though a team might let a player go, there was always some way the team could get something out of it. I think the Cowboys were so desperate to get rid of me that they accepted something like $100 from the Patriots. It wasn't much, but I guess it was something the Cowboys had to do since they weren't letting me play or paying me, and they were saying I wasn't on the team even though I technically was.

Chuck Fairbanks had come in as head coach of the Patriots only the year before. I was happy enough to be there, but by the time I arrived, I was flat broke. I went to Fairbanks the first thing and told him, "Look, I need $5,000. I don't have any money, and I don't have anything here."

He said, "I'm not going to give you any money," and I told him, "Well, in that case, I'm going back to Texas. I might be broke, but at least I'll be broke in my home state." So he went on and gave me $5,000 and let me play.

I used some of the money to rent a little two-bedroom apartment in Hyde Park. While I lived there, an antibussing race riot happened only two blocks away, though I didn't know it was going on until later because I was at practice. But it was ironic that I'd moved right into the middle of an area of racial tension. All I could do was shake my head, but I wasn't too surprised. Boston was almost as prejudiced as the Deep South. I'd go out looking for someone to spend some time with, but there weren't too many blacks in Boston.

Since I was still recovering from the operation to my right knee and my left knee still needed surgery, you might think that Fairbanks would have taken it easy with me at first, but he did just the opposite. He threw me into the fire. Instead of having me play one of the linebacker positions, he had me playing wide receiver on special teams covering kickoffs and punts. I'd never played wide receiver, which is a position that requires a lot of speed, and the first week of practice, I couldn't push all that hard. I was running down the ball, but I couldn't get away from the defensive backs. I concentrated on doing that in practice, and by our second game, all of a sudden, I had a burst of speed. I thought, *God bless, I seem to have another gear.*

After that, I was able to outrun most defensive backs. I mean, I was flying. To tell the truth, though, I hated playing in cold weather. I wrapped up as much as I could, but I never could get used to the cold. As if it wasn't bad enough being cold all day, after practice I had to put ice packs on my muscles and joints to prevent inflammation. But as I've made obvious, if I was on the field, I was going to do something good for the team, and I wasn't about to let the cold slow me down. During the second game, I made two big plays. In one, I hit my opponent when he was trying to catch the ball, causing a fumble recovery. In the other, against the Pittsburgh Steelers, Lynn Swann came down the middle, and I made him fumble, giving us a chance to win the game and putting us in the playoffs.

By game three, Fairbanks had taken note of my skills and drive and made me cocaptain. That might have shocked my teammates, but it didn't shock me because I'd always been motivated to go where I wanted in terms of play on the field. If the guys on the line did their job, then

I would make something happen. They might not have trusted me at first because I still had a lot to learn—especially that the eye in the sky was watching me, trying to figure out how to most effectively use my skills and quickness.

They had me playing mostly on special teams, so at least I was playing, but there was some good and bad to that. Because I was playing positions other than linebacker, I had to learn how to tone down and do stuff that I hadn't done before. It might have been good for me up to a point, but playing those other positions so much worried me a little. I wasn't playing defense, and if you're a defensive player and you're not playing defense, you're not practicing defense, and you're going to get rusty and lose your game. That's what was beginning to happen to me, so maybe the most important thing I had to learn was how to turn lemons into lemonade.

During one game in which I played middle linebacker, we went into the huddle, and I was trying to call the next play, but there was this defensive end who was talking to somebody else and wasn't paying attention. This guy was about 6'5" and 280, but that didn't matter to me. If I had to get in somebody's face—not to be tough but to be heard because that was my job—that's what I did. It wasn't that I thought I could whup everybody, but I was willing to give it my best shot if I had to. That's the way linebackers are. So I grabbed him, dragged him to the huddle, and chewed him out.

He started cussing me out and huffing and puffing like he was about to whip up on me right then and there. Before he could do anything, though, we broke the huddle and went to make the play. And what did he do but go right in and make a sack, hitting the quarterback in the backfield. And who was the first person to run up and congratulate him? Me. That really baffled him. He looked at me like I was crazy, but he wasn't understanding my job. As middle linebacker, it was my job to get the defense to play and play well. Then he came back the very next play and sacked the quarterback again.

It's funny how you can use other people's adrenaline, energy, and talent to push a team forward, and I was good at that. In this case, our little argument ramped up his aggression, which was then directed at the other team. You just have to know how to push the right buttons. The thing was, I didn't have any fear of even the biggest guys even though they could have kicked my butt. That came from charging big guys like that and getting in their face on the field. Some players accept that, but others will fight you. There are more locker room fights than you realize. In the end, though, it all comes down to how much you want to win and how hard you want to play.

Toward the end of the season, when we flew down to Miami to play the Dolphins, I thought everything was going pretty well. That feeling continued after Fairbanks called me to his room and said, "Rodrigo, I know you need another operation on your leg, but next year, I want you on my team. Think about that."

I said, "Coach, I'd love to be on your team if you're going to give me an opportunity to start. My only problem with Dallas is that they were being ridiculous about the whole thing. We're playing sports, not protect your buddy's job, and sooner or later, the guy on top has got to move over and let the next guy come up."

If Fairbanks was going to be protecting some players and holding back others, well, that wasn't for me. I knew my game wasn't going to last that long—maybe six more years at my top form. After the age of thirty, your game just isn't going to stay at the top. You might be able to play line or tight end because, while you have to be good, your skills don't have to be as sharp. But when you're playing running back, wide receiver, linebacker, and quarterback, you can't lose a step. I told Fairbanks, "You haven't seen anything yet. Can you imagine me playing a whole season behind a decent line? Man, come on. I put on a show."

So he said, "Okay."

After the season was over, I had the operation on my left knee, and the next season, I came back to training camp, which was at the University of Massachusetts at Amherst. I'd worked out hard during the off season, so I was in pretty good shape, considering back-to-back operations. One day during practice, all were doing their times in the 40-yard dash. You might remember the little contest between Calvin Hill and me while I was with the Cowboys, which was that standard 40.

Anyway, we usually ran one or two 40s, though a lot of players didn't like to do it because they didn't want to overextend themselves. The guys who were really fast, though, didn't mind since it was one way to show what they were about. Guys often think that flat-out speed is going to make a difference because speed is what gets people to look at you with raised eyebrows. But your speed during a game is usually a little different than in practice because of the adrenaline. Plus, during a game, you don't usually run flat out in a straight line for very far.

While we were waiting to run, we're all doing our thing to prepare, and I could hear one of my teammates praying. He wasn't shouting it out, but he was praying loudly enough for the rest of us to hear, and what he was asking for was that he'd do his run in good time, that he wouldn't stumble, and so forth. But when he got up there, he immediately stumbled and fell. So he asked for a second chance, and his shoe popped off. Then he begged for a third chance, and that didn't work out either, and his time was terrible. Everything he'd prayed not to happen did. It was kind of sad but funny, too, since I'd never seen anybody pray for something and have every one of those prayers turn into its opposite—within minutes. Maybe the incident illustrates that old quest of mine to learn not only *how* or *when* to pray but *why*.

But then it was my turn, and even though I'd been praying, too, I'd tightened up while I was waiting, and I did my run in something like 4.7 seconds, which wasn't good. I was disappointed, so after the other guys ran, I came back for my own second chance, and this time I did a little better at 4.5.

Training camp went well enough, but during the preseason, the Patriots and the New York Jets, who had a famous rivalry, refused to play because the players felt that the owners were not dealing with them in good faith. The players were negotiating a new contract, and they thought that a strike would bring public attention to the issue and force the owners to sit down with the players. Once the strike was over, all the Players Association people, like Irwin Cross and Earl Morrall, who was the Dolphins' quarterback and the leader of the Players Association, went on TV and said, "There will be no retaliation against any of the Patriots' or the Jets' players who are allegedly behind the strike." Yeah, right. I was one of those saying we should strike, so you can guess whom they blamed everything on.

After that, we had one more preseason game before the last cut. I might have been nervous considering the way I was being blamed for the strike, but they didn't cut me. Instead, they cut an inside linebacker behind me. But the news wasn't all good. At the time, New England played two linebackers inside and two outside. Sam Hunt and Steve Nelson were on the inside, and Steve Zabel and Steve King were on the outside. I was playing behind Nelson, and the Patriots drafted Rod Shoate from Oklahoma to play the weak side behind Sam Hunt. All through training camp and preseason, I was blowing up guys and making plays and interceptions and so forth. But when it came down to who was going to start for the first game of the regular season, it wasn't me.

Man, was I disappointed. I thought I'd proved myself and that I deserved to start, and so did a lot of people watching me. Even Fairbanks had said I could start, so I could only conclude that I'd been set up again. They lied to me, just like in the Cowboys. I went to Fairbanks and said, "Hey, what's up?"

And he said, "What I want you to do is just to be the best special team player we have out there and be ready to start at any time."

I said, "Okay," and tried to make the adjustment. After all, I was cocaptain, and there was that lemons and lemonade thing.

Then we played our first game—a home game—against the Houston Oilers. Even though we didn't win, it was a good game, and I got to play. After the game, though, the linebacker they'd cut came to me and said, "You know, Rodrigo, they told me to hang around." Then he looked at me in a way that said they'd told him to hang around because they were going to cut another linebacker. I guess I should have been worried, but I'd made the team, signed a two-year contract with a little bonus, gotten my paycheck, and was cocaptain. I thought I was in solid. I'd found a place to stay, bought some furniture, and got set up, thinking I'd be around for a while. But now, there was this guy telling me this, and I thought, *Wow.* I pondered it a little bit, but I couldn't wrap my head around what might be going down.

The following week, we were getting ready to play the Cowboys in a home game. I was really geared up for that. Back then, when you played a home game, the fans in the home city didn't get to see the game on TV unless it was sold out. The only folks who got to see the game were the ones who went to it in person. But when you played a road game, everybody back home gets to see the game broadcast. That meant that everybody in Dallas—including my family—would get to see me play against the team that had dissed me. The Cowboys might have thought I'd be out for revenge, but really, they didn't want to face me because my game was on point. Even if I was playing on special teams, I was blowing up the opposition.

The thing was, I couldn't figure out why the Patriots weren't going to let me start. Then, just a few days before the game, it all became crystal clear. I came to practice only to have Fairbanks tell me I'm cut. I said, "What?" He didn't give me any reason but just turned around and walked off. We'd talked several times in the past, and if there were any problems, they should have been brought up then. But he didn't try to explain because he didn't have a good explanation. On later reflection, I thought that it probably wasn't his decision but one that had been made over his head. Maybe it was a case of retaliation for my participation in the strike, but if it was, Fairbanks couldn't explain it that way, so he didn't even try. He wasn't in the habit of being personable with his players anyway, and I guess he was just trying to do the owners' dirty work as painlessly as possible.

I was hurt. It might not have been so bad if I hadn't been cocaptain. And now I could see why they weren't going to let me start. They weren't going to let me play at all. I was out, flat on my butt, and they played the game without me. I couldn't believe it, and I couldn't help but wonder what was happening to me. But no one—not the Players Association, owners, coaches, or players—would admit to anything. Suddenly everyone was like an ostrich with its head buried in the sand. The statement that the Patriots gave in the papers was "No comment." That meant "Use your imagination," because they didn't have any legitimate reason to cut me.

The long and short of it was that the owners weren't going to tolerate the strike, and even though they'd claimed there would be no retaliation, they bagged me up. The Players Association didn't support me, and since I wasn't famous, nobody gave a darn. We'd struck, and the quarterbacks had turned on the other players by going back into camp, and the other players caved in, so nobody was supporting anybody else. After that, I completely lost faith in the Players Association. I wouldn't waste a nickel or a minute listening to anything they had to say because it was just a sellout organization.

But there might have been another reason for the exact timing of the cut. I still had a few friends out there, and one of them was Billy Joe DuPree, who was still with the Cowboys. He called me with some disturbing news. At a meeting right before the game, Landry told the Cowboy players not to worry about me because I wasn't going to be playing. When I heard that, I thought, Oh yeah. Now it makes sense. It was a tenth-round set-up, and the Cowboys' footprint was all over it.

And guess how that all went down with the Cowboy players? They all got tight enough to fit through the eye of a needle because they saw how the owners and the Players Association could work together to destroy a player they didn't like, no matter how well he played. And it was no secret in the league that I was playing well. It was a bad situation that was about to get dire as my termination sent me into an economic tailspin. I'd come to Boston with nothing, and expecting a paycheck, I'd spent the $5,000 that Fairbanks had given me to rent an apartment and buy furniture, dishes, groceries, and so forth. I mean, I was broke. I think I had about $100, and only a week remained before the next month's rent was due.

I stayed in my apartment for a couple of lonely days, just hoping somebody would pick me up, but there was nothing. It was the beginning of the season, so all the teams were set, and none of them were interested in adding another player. When you get cut in the last round, you're pretty much done unless somebody deliberately keeps a spot open in case you become available. You might get picked up then if you're one of the best among those who were cut, but it's also true that teams don't want to pay those guys anything, either. But at least you'd be playing. If you get cut one or two games into the season, you don't stand a chance unless somebody gets hurt.

Then, a few days into the week, I got a phone call from an NFL representative who said he wanted to meet with me. I said okay. We met at a restaurant, and I went there thinking they wanted to send me somewhere while I got past this situation, which wasn't my fault though everybody blamed me. The NFL did want to send me somewhere, but it wasn't anyplace I wanted to be.

"Go to Canada and play this year," they said, "and we'll pay your salary. Next year, you have to stay in Canada, but your salary will go down to the Canadian salary." Well, the Canadian salary was something like $37,000 a year, which was a lot less than was being paid to players in the US by then.

I asked them, "If I go to Canada this year and get that out of the way, can I come back to the NFL next year instead of staying in Canada?"

And they said, "No. If you take this deal, you can never come back to the NFL." Well, I couldn't accept that sort of offer because it was really no offer at all. If I took it, I'd be falling into the same old trap of self-denial that all the other guys were stuck in.

I thought, *Well, I love football, but I have a life. I might have to eat beans and cornbread, but I'm still going to be me.* But my self–pep talks didn't change the fact that I was pretty dejected after that meeting. I hoped that someone would come through and help find justice for the situation, but as I sat there, alone in my apartment, no one did. And when the week was up, I had to get out of there. I packed up my car and headed back to Texas. Along the way, I stopped in New York City to hang out with a friend of mine, then I drove to Jackson, Mississippi, and hung out for a little while with another friend. Then I drove on to Dallas.

I might have been back in Texas, but my problems only got worse. No sooner did I arrive in Dallas than the fan blades in my car came loose for some reason and tore up my radiator. Now, not only was I broke and without a job or a place to live, but I didn't even have a car. I left the car at a repair shop even though I had no idea when or how I'd be able to pay for the repairs. I had just enough money left to get a hotel room. At eight o'clock the next morning, I called Billy Joe DuPree.

"Look," I told him. "I'm in Dallas, man. My car broke down, and I'm broke too. I need to get my car fixed so I can go back to Houston to see what I can do to get myself together."

He said, "Okay, Rod. We have a meeting at nine, and I'll come by after that." He came by and paid for my car repairs so I could get out of there. That was a tremendous help during a trying time. It was great to see Billy Joe again, too, though we didn't really talk about my problems. We both knew what had happened, and it was pointless to go into it all. And he had a game to play.

After my car was repaired, I drove to Houston. There, I found a place to live for a short time thanks to a friend of mine, John Hightower, who was a real estate guy. He had some houses that were vacant, and he let me stay in one that wasn't yet occupied. I was there for a couple of weeks, trying to get myself together and deal with all the stuff and confusion surrounding me. But life goes on, and you have to figure it out. I tried to find a job, but nobody wanted to do anything for me. Rice people hated me. Al Conover was still coaching at Rice, and he's the guy who told the pro owners not to draft me because I was a troublemaker. And the university itself still didn't like me because I'd made them do things they didn't want to do. Plus, I had an unpaid student loan, so they wouldn't release my transcripts. Without those, I couldn't even look for a decent job outside pro sports. Everybody else hated me too. I wasn't getting any love from anybody anywhere. It was a terrible, bleak time.

When some players get cut and have nothing else they can do besides play football, they sometimes turn to selling drugs or other illegal activities to make enough money to stay afloat. They get a couple of grand together and start dealing because they still know a lot of players and other people who will buy. But that was something I didn't want to do, and besides, I didn't know anything about that kind of stuff. Nor was I going to let something like that trip me up. I intended to stay out of trouble and get back to playing football.

Finally, it seemed like I might be able to do that. I struck a deal to play with the Charlotte Hornets, a World Football League team. I got a little money from them, but that opportunity failed to materialize. The WFL had problems, and it just fell apart, ceasing operations in the middle of 1975. After that, the Patriots agreed to sign me again, but they waived me before the season even began.

I felt like a bouncing football, taking crazy hops all over the place. Or maybe it was more like golf since I always seemed to get knocked toward one hole after another. And now, it looked like I was at the bottom of the deepest one, trying to make it out. But before the despair grew too deep, someone miraculously lowered a ladder down to me. With five games to go in the season, Don Shula, head coach of the Miami Dolphins, called and wanted me to play with them. They didn't have a good linebacker, and Shula remembered how I'd lit up Larry

Csonka in that preseason game while I was still with the Cowboys. The invitation was all I needed, and I was off to play for the Dolphins.

CHAPTER 13

THE MIAMI DOLPHINS

The Miami Dolphins were reloading at the time because they didn't have the team they needed. Even so, they still had a couple of good players and a chance to go to the playoffs, which excited me. I flew to Miami, worked out for them, and did a physical, which, of course, focused on my knees. They solved my knee problems with two surgeries, but I had to sign a waiver stating that if something happened to either of my knees, they wouldn't be on the hook. After that, I joined the team, hoping to get a chance to play. I was grateful that they carried me for the time they did because everything I'd planned had gone south and everything I'd thought would happen had passed me by. I was riding on fumes from year to year, hoping I'd get another shot to play, but things didn't look promising. Like the Dolphins, I needed reloading.

As a city, Miami wasn't about too much back then. It was more of a business environment than a social one. Even so, the population was very diverse, with whites, blacks, Hispanics, and people from the Caribbean, but it also was very segregated. Each group occupied its own neighborhoods, and overall, black people were not well respected, though the door was open to those with money.

Considering what had happened to me the last year, it's no surprise that I was still broke. Thankfully, Andre Tillman let me stay with him.

Andre was a tight end from Texas Tech, about 6'4" and 230 pounds. He was tall and lanky for a football player, but he was a great athlete with great hands—just an exceptional player. His brother also was in and out of camp. I'd run across him with the Cowboys and the Patriots. It seemed like every camp I went to, he was there, too, trying to make the team.

Before head coach Don Shula joined the Dolphins in 1970, the tide had been going out for the team. Afterward, though, it came back in strong. Shula had played pro ball for several teams and had been the coach of the Baltimore Colts before the Dolphins' owner, Joe Robbie, convinced him to go to Miami.

Larry Csonka had left the team the year before, which might have been a benefit to me. I didn't know if he was the type to hold a grudge, but I had been one of the few guys able to stop him cold. But even without Csonka, the offense still had some great players whom I got to practice with. Quarterback Bob Griese was one of those. Under him, the Dolphins went to the Super Bowl three times in a row, winning two of them. He was a six-time Pro Bowler and two-time All-Pro, and he'd been named the NFL's Most Valuable Player while I was in college. But in my first game with the Dolphins, he broke his big toe, putting him out for the remainder of the season. A broken big toe might not seem like a serious injury, but for a football player who constantly has to push off from the feet, the big toe is very important. Griese's backup was Earl Morrall. He was the same guy who'd said that there would be no repercussions from the strike. I guess he was close to forty at the time.

Hall of Famer Larry Little was at offensive guard. He was a two-time Super Bowl champion and a five-time Pro Bowler and All-Pro and was later named to the NFL 1970s All-Decade Team. He went on to serve as head coach at Bethune-Cookman University in Daytona Beach, where he'd played college ball, and after that, head coach at North Carolina Central University.

Another guard was Bob Kuechenberg, who was a Pro Bowler, All-Pro, and two-time Super Bowl champ. Football must have been in his blood since his brother, Rudy, played for the Chicago Bears. Bob could be a complainer and a holder of grudges, and I'm not the only one to say that. All-Pro Jason Taylor, who played for pro ball from 1997 to 2011, mostly for Miami, had this to say about Bob's perennial complaints about his past teams: "It's another chapter in the grumpy Kuechenberg story. It's Kuechenberg. He gets up every year and complains about something. If it ain't one thing, it's another. He needs a hug and a hobby." Jim Langer was the center, and he's generally considered to be one of the all-time greats in that position. He was with the Dolphins' in their three Super Bowl appearances and two wins. That includes Super Bowl VII, when the team not only won the game but went into it with an unbeaten and untied season—itself an NFL record. His great playing earned him multiple All-Pro honors and Pro Bowl appearances, and he also was named to the NFL 1970s All-Decade Team.

At offensive tackle, we had Norm Evans and Wayne Moore. Both were Pro Bowlers and two-time Super Bowl champs. In fact, just about the whole offensive line had made All-Pro or the Hall of Fame at one time or another. Miami's offense also had tight end Andre Tillman, whom I've already mentioned, and some good running backs. One of the receivers, Nat Moore, was a Pro Bowler and a first-team All-Pro. He was famous for a reception during a game with the New York Jets, where he was hit from both sides at once, sending him spinning around in the air. That became known as "the helicopter catch," but that was after my time. Another wide receiver was Howard Twilley, a two-time Super Bowl champ.

So we had an excellent offense, but truthfully, the defense wasn't too hot. The defensive line couldn't put pressure on anybody, and all the linebackers were either rookies or older guys. Because of that, the Dolphins' defense had earned the nickname "the No-Name Defense."

Shula was kind of hard on me from day one, but what was new about having a head coach be hard on me? I was more interested in the play, and being second string, I had a chance to practice with the best of the best and work on my game. Like I've said before, I was rough and tough on the field, and while some of the guys took it in stride, other guys didn't like it much and would get mad and try to hurt me.

Kuechenberg was one of those. He didn't like me much anyway, and on top of that, he didn't like it that I could get away from him. The first few times he tried to hurt me, I blew it off as no big thing. But it kept happening, and finally, he tried to run up behind me to knock me out. I spied him out of the corner of my eye and pivoted, and he sailed on by and fell flat on his face. Soon after, another player confided, "That was no accident. Kuechenberg was trying to take you out. He's embarrassed because you were making plays on him." That's when I learned that Kuechenberg is the type of guy who'll try to take revenge if you embarrass him. Well, I'd been dealing with that kind of stuff since I was a kid, and I didn't mind him trying. I just kept doing my thing to him took pride in making those plays. I might not get a chance to show everybody what I could do, but I could demonstrate my skills to some of the best, and the Dolphins' offense knew I had game.

As we went into my second week there, I planned to show Shula all my stuff, but that didn't happen. In my first game, which was against the Buffalo Bills, I was playing special team, and in making a play, I came down with all my weight on one leg. My foot slid then hung up on the artificial turf, jamming the muscle along my tibia and rupturing it. Back then, we didn't get checked out all that much by doctors, and that was especially true with Miami. The ruptured muscle didn't immediately swell up. It took a couple of weeks to do that, so at first you really couldn't tell from looking that the muscle was ruptured. But it was extremely painful, and I couldn't do anything. Putting pressure on it hurt, and running was impossible, so for almost three weeks out of the five weeks I was there, I was just hobbling up and down the field.

Shula might have thought I was faking it because he couldn't see the swelling that first week or so. He asked me if I could play. Being the player I was, I said, "Yeah, Coach. I'm ready to go." What else could I say? If you were one of the black players and wanted to keep playing, you had to play no matter where you were or what might be wrong with you. So I did my practice, went to the games, and did what I was supposed to do. After the third week, I healed, and in another week, I was flying around, back to my old self.

The truth is, Shula was the kind of coach who had no hesitation about sending out injured players. Andre Tillman was an exceptional player, and he could have been a great player, but he also injured his knee, and Shula ruined him by forcing him to go out and play on one leg. I don't think Andre ever played on a good knee because he never got a chance to heal. That was sad because Andre was great, and even though he was just hobbling, he was still making plays and catching a few passes. But he couldn't really do much and was getting hurt all the time because of the injury he already had. The way Shula pressured him seemed inhumane to me.

Despite the injuries, we still had a chance to make the playoffs, down to the last game of the season, against the Colts. This was before they moved to Indianapolis, and they were still in Baltimore. I was in good condition for that game and came on strong, but our defense just wasn't making the plays. Baltimore was running the ball quite a bit, and I was supposed to go in there and stop them, but I didn't do it. Maybe I'd grown a little slack because I figured I wasn't going to be with Miami after that year anyway. Shula didn't seem to care too much for African American players, though I think he was okay with superstars because they kept him going. I also think he wasn't concentrating enough on defense.

Anyway, the team we were counting on to win lost, so we were out of the running. That was the first time that the Dolphins hadn't made the playoffs since Shula took over. After that, I left Miami and went back Houston. I discovered, though, that while I might be back at home, I was far from settled. To my lack of surprise, during the off season, the Dolphins traded me to the St. Louis Cardinals. Actually, they sold me to the Cardinals for $100.

I was at Rice University, working out, when the deal went down. A scout for St. Louis came by to view some of the Rice players. I'd already done my workout and was playing basketball in the gym, and the scout saw me and called me over to tell me he was thinking about sending me to the Cardinals' camp. I told him, "I'll do a deal with you." So I went to the St. Louis camp in 1976, and that was the end of my time with Miami. All in all, I'd been with the Cowboys for a year and a half, the New England Patriots for six or seven games, and the Miami Dolphins for five games. And now that I'd been picked up by the Cardinals, I couldn't help but wonder how that would pan out.

CHAPTER

14

THE ST. LOUIS CARDINALS

The St. Louis Cardinals began playing in 1960 but moved to Tempe, Arizona, in 1987 to become the Arizona Cardinals. They'd had a miserable season the year before I joined—enough so that they were beginning to be called the "Cardiac Cardinals" for their stalls during the season. One perfect example was the playoff game against the LA Rams in Los Angeles Memorial Coliseum. Rams' player Lawrence McCutcheon rushed for a total of 202 yards, setting an NFL playoff record, and Jack Youngblood and Bill Simpson intercepted way too many Cardinals' passes.

The problem with the Cardinals wasn't the offense. Our head coach, Don Coryell, was known as "Air Coryell" because of his strong and innovative passing offense. He also is the first coach to win more than one hundred games in both collegiate and pro football. He was with the Cardinals for about five years, and after that, he moved to San Diego Chargers, where he finished out his coaching career and was inducted into the Chargers Hall of Fame.

As you can imagine from that minibiography, the team had a great offensive line, and it had been kicking the defense's butt for years. Pretty much everybody there was All-Pro and had been to the Pro Bowl. Quarterback Jim Hart was a real nice guy, and he was an accurate passer, but he couldn't take any heat. He was kind of like Tom

Brady. If you put some heat on him, his game just fell apart. But also like Brady, if he had some protection, he could throw that football. I'm not trying to take anything away from Brady, who is a great player and won his fair share of Super Bowls. But if you put some heat on him up the middle and make him move out of the pocket, he's at a loss because he isn't a great rollout quarterback. He's probably the best quarterback in the League, but even great players have their weaknesses. I never have understood why his opponents don't just punch up the middle and get him off his spot. That's what the teams that beat him did. So the Cardinals' offensive line was pretty good, and opponents had to blitz them to get to Hart. If they did that, and he thought he was going to get hit, he'd flinch or clench up. A player's intentions might be good, and he might think he's ready to be hit, but his body might be saying, "No, I'm not." In football, your body is trained to withstand physical punishment, and when you're young, you usually can overcome your reaction to fear and take the hit. My job was to run into guys who weigh 300 pounds—not to wait for them but to attack them. Through experience, I learned how to approach certain guys and put myself in the best position to hit and weaken them and make them give up not only the ball but the competitive spirit, all while I was protecting myself.

But there's a limit to accepting that sort of punishment, and it takes a lot of macho for a quarterback to stand in the pocket, waiting to make a pass with a bunch of really big guys running at him. After you've been in the league for a while, when you see that sort of weight and power bearing down on you, your body will cringe. It happens in a lot of positions. You'll see receivers looking around and dropping passes they never used to drop. You'll see quarterbacks who, instead of standing up in the pocket, will fold up so they won't get hit hard. The anticipation of the pain takes over, and your body, instead of reacting the way you want, will do something to protect itself from the pain. It's not something you want to happen. It's an involuntary reaction that happens because you know you're about to get hurt.

That reaction is bad for any player, but it's especially bad for offensive players because when it takes over, all they can do is be defensive. It's also why teams that regularly rotate their players generally play better. All players get to stay in practice and keep from getting rusty, but they also to rest a little so they don't have to keep taking punishment without a break. Teams that play their starters most of the time will see their players' physical health and fighting spirit start to break down. When shying away from taking the licks starts becoming a regular occurrence, you know it's time to get out of the game because your body's quit and you no longer have the mentality to push past the big hits to make the plays. Well, Jim Hart didn't have that mentality. He just couldn't take the punishment anymore, and if he was going to get hit, he was going to fold up. But if he didn't have any pressure on him, his passes would tear you up. He was a great passer.

Right in the middle of the offensive line was center Tom Banks. He'd played for the Auburn Tigers in College, and during his time with the Cardinals, he racked up four Pro Bowls. Two-time Pro Bowler Bob Young was at guard. Bob, along with the other Cardinal offensive linemen, was the guy who established modern weight lifting as an element of NFL training.

Conrad Dobler was at right guard. He was one nasty player, and he reveled in his reputation. He once said, "I see defensive linemen jump to knock a pass down. When that happened near me, I'd smack 'em in the solar plexus, and that got their hands down real quick." That didn't mean he was a bad player, just a *bad* player. Dobler was featured on the cover of *Sports Illustrated* under the headline "Pro Football's Dirtiest Player." Sportswriter Paul Zimmerman, better known as Dr. Z, reportedly said, "Conrad Dobler was mean dirty. He tried to hurt people in a bad way (but) he made teams that he played on better. He played hurt, didn't complain, but he was a filthy, filthy player."

Left tackle was Roger Finnie. He'd played college ball for Florida A&M. Six-time Pro Bowler Dan Dierdorf started every game at right tackle and was another standout player. A six-time Pro Bowler, he also was selected five times as first-team All-Pro. He later became a sportscaster for ABC and CBS and won the Pete Rozelle Radio-Television Award from the Pro Football Hall of Fame in 2008.

Wide receiver Mel Gray was a first-team All-Pro and a three-time Pro Bowler, though he went for a fourth the year after I left the Cardinals. Our running backs were three-time Pro Bowler Terry Metcalf and Pro Bowler Jim Otis. Jim's best year was probably the one before I joined the Cardinals, when he rushed for 1,076 yards.

Jackie Smith was an All-Pro tight end. He also was a five-time Pro Bowler, so he'd been a pretty good player, but that didn't last. He retired in 1977 or 1978, but the next year, Tom Landry convinced him to join the Cowboys. When the Cowboys went to the Super Bowl that year against the Pittsburgh Steeler, the Cowboys' management must not have wanted to give Billy Joe DuPree the chance to shine even though he'd been playing tight end all along. In typical fashion, Landry forsook a solid player to put in a guy who was new to the team to try to make him the hero. It was a foolish move in my view because DuPree and Staubach had been working well together for five or so years and had their timing down pat.

But apparently that didn't matter to Landry. In the third quarter, he took out DuPree and sent in Smith to catch the winning pass, but unfortunately for the Cowboys, the substitution didn't work out as planned. Smith was wide-open in the end zone when Roger Staubach fired off the pass. It wasn't an easy catch, but it was one you'd expect a Pro Bowler to make. Instead, Smith slipped on a wet spot on the turf, throwing him off position. The ball hit him in the face, and he dropped it. It might not have been the decisive factor in the Cowboys' loss to the Steelers, but the play became infamous, and Smith retired permanently after that season. Landry should have kept DuPree in play, but no, he just had to pull DuPree and put in Smith.

As I said, the Cardinals' defense wasn't too hot—average or below. We had a few good players but not enough for every position. One of the greats was cornerback Roger Wehrli. Staubach once said of him, "The term 'Shutdown Corner' originated with Roger Wehrli. I never played with a better cornerback. You had to be aware of him all the time." He was a seven-time Pro Bowler and a five-time first team All-Pro. So I was in the St. Louis camp, practicing with the big boys and doing my thing against them every day. And I was doing well—at least I thought I was. Our preseason games were against the Chicago Bears, the San Diego Chargers, the Oakland Raiders, and the Denver Broncos. We played San Diego in Tokyo, Japan. The NFL was interested in taking American football overseas, and this was the first try at that.

Tokyo is a very crowded city with people living on top of each other, but it also was very orderly and clean, with police on every corner. The people were warm on the outside and very enthusiastic and expressive. They also were extremely polite. If they asked you for an autograph, they'd always give you a little gift in return. But they didn't socialize with us much, and black people were obviously scarce in Japan and pretty much insignificant. We were there for nine or ten days, and we got a chance to sightsee around Tokyo and to visit Yokohama. A lot of the married players took their wives. Getting to visit another part of the world was good experience for me.

I got to start in that game, and we won it. Then, after we returned home, it was time for the last cut. We had this defensive tackle named Larry Jameson. A free agent, he was a big old country boy who was the Cardinals' sixth-round draft pick that year. He was my roommate in camp, and we rolled for three or four weeks, and I worked hard against him in practice, but at 6'8" and 295 pounds, he was just a monster. None of the guys could handle him: not Banks, not even badass Dobler. Heck, two-on-one they couldn't handle him. And when he stood up, quarterbacks had a hard time throwing over him. But I don't think he got to play more than one or two preseason games before they suddenly let him go. I couldn't understand why they'd cut a guy who was that big and strong and whom nobody could block. I guess Coryell preferred first-round draft pick Mike Dawson. Dawson was a good kid, but he wasn't Jameson.

So it wasn't just black players who got cut for mysterious reasons. It could happen to anybody, and then, of course, it was my turn. When I was informed that I was out, I couldn't believe it. In retrospect, I made a bad choice in hiring this agent out of Houston to represent me and try to negotiate a new contract. I think he went in there and talked noise or asked for too much money and annoyed them trying to be a hotshot lawyer and agent. He didn't understand that this wasn't court; it was a negotiation. I thought I'd be included in the negotiations and get asked what I wanted. If that had happened, we probably would have had a deal, but I think my agent turned them off or they wanted another deal or a combination of both. I'm not sure since I was on the outside the negotiations, but whatever it was, I was out. In the end, I could only blame myself for using a rookie agent to represent me.

As I was leaving the facility, I told Jim Hart, Terry Metcalf, and some of the other guys on the offensive line that I'd been cut. They started laughing and saying things like, "Hey, man, quit joking around."

I said, "No, Coryell just cut me. I'm outta here." I left very dejected. I'd started in all but one of the preseason games, and I thought I was going to start once the regular season began, but there I was, cut once again. It was very disappointing. Soon after, though, the general manager for the New York Giants called me and asked me to fly up for a look at. I forget his name, but he was an older man who'd had been with the team for years and years. I packed my bags, went to New York, and did a workout in their camp. I wasn't at my best, but I did okay, and I thought I might get to play for them, but they decided not to take me.

The general manager told me, "Man, I don't know what to say. I sent for you, and I want you, but Arnsparger says no." Bill Arnsparger was the head coach, but he was only with the Giants for a couple of years. That was the totality of his career as the head coach for a pro team, though he served in other coaching positions in the pros and as head coach of several college teams.

Rejected once more, I went back to Houston. Waco was out of the question. There wasn't anything in the way of work for me there, and all I could do in Waco was get in trouble. In Houston, I had a few friends I could hang out with, and I figured I could make it there. I still had a little money, so for the time being, I was okay financially, but to make sure I didn't run out of funds, I did some freelance training sessions and helped several players take care of business and errands they didn't have time to do themselves. I insisted on maintaining some sort of employment, and I was honored to help my fellow athletes. All that time, I was still looking for a job in football, but my prospects seemed bleak. St. Louis had cut me in the last game of the preseason, which was a bad time for that to happen because, as I mentioned earlier, by then, all the teams already had their lineups.

Even so, there were trickles of interest. By the time the league was four or five games into the season, I called up Houston Oilers scout Tom Williams and asked him for an interview. He said yes, so I went to talk to him. He didn't say anything one way or another, but he did ask if I wanted to work out with them. I put on my workout clothes and went out there, and they had a running back run some plays with me. I wasn't sure what they wanted me to do—tackle the guy or knock down or intercept passes—so I didn't do any of that but just kept up with him stride for stride to show that I could have knocked the ball down or caught it. We ran about twenty plays like that and did some agility work. When it was all over, they said, "Well, Rodrigo, we have our roster filled right now, and we just don't have a place for you. But we think that you're a good athlete, and if we get an opening, we'd like to have you."

I said, "Okay," but I left as dejected as before. Finding opportunities is tough, and it doesn't get any easier after that. Even if you are picked up by a team, some other player—probably some brother—is probably going to lose his job. That's the way they did back then. So it was a bleak time, and it was all I could do to keep my head together.

I went home and hung around, but that—and my dejection—didn't last long. The very next day, Al Davis, principal owner and manager of the Oakland Raiders, called to tell me he wanted to fly me out there. I told him I'd love to play for the Raiders.

Here I go again, I thought as I prepared to leave Houston. Filled with determination, I packed my bags as though I was about to sign a contract and flew out to Oakland.

CHAPTER

15

SUPER BOWL BOUND

By the time I arrived in Oakland, the Raiders had already played something like seven games. I was put through a physical, the same as with the other teams. That went fine, but when it came to contracts, Al Davis was as cheap or cheaper than the Cowboys had been, especially for black players who weren't superstars. I ended up getting only $2,000 a game. It wasn't a good situation, but I didn't have a choice. I wanted to play, they had a good team, and I liked the Raiders. As a matter of fact, when I came out of college, the Raiders had been my first choice and the Cowboys my second.

But Al bought players as cheaply as he could, and I was disappointed by that. He had an attitude of "Let's win," and that was good, but as far as the way he treated the players, maybe one or two of them made out okay financially, but the rest of us didn't do all that well. Also remember that in California, you're paying state as well as federal taxes, and the team was in the Bay Area, which is an expensive place to live. But most of the players weren't making any money. That was ridiculous, and I wasn't the only one unhappy about the pay. Skip Thomas, our star defensive back, was covering all the speedy wide receivers and holding it down, but it seemed he'd signed a messed-up contract, and Al wouldn't make adjustments. Skip was hot about that and cussed Al every day.

But all that didn't mean that Davis wasn't good for the team in a number of ways. When he was hired in 1962 as the Raiders' head coach and general manager, he was only thirty-three, which made him the youngest head coach in pro football history. The team, which was only a few years old, was at the bottom of the barrel, but Davis plucked them out of it with some good hires and by utilizing an aggressive offensive strategy. His motto was "Just win, baby."

One of his hires was Big John Madden, who'd mentored as a coach under Don Coryell—the same coach who'd fired me just months earlier. Madden started with the Raiders as the defensive coach, but when I joined the team, he was head coach. He served in that capacity for ten years, and during that time, he never had a losing season. Maybe that was because of the way he treated the players during practice. As was usual, the first-string offense worked out against the second-string defense, and the first-string defense worked out against the second-string offense, but the two groups alternated days for heavy practice. That was sensible because it gave the players a chance to rest a little on their off days. Some teams practice everyone constantly, which tends to wear down the players. Their coaches don't seem to understand that players are men, not machines, and you can't run them all the time. People need to recuperate. To my way of thinking, Madden had the right idea about practice.

The Raiders' offense was pure dynamite—tough and hard-hitting—and so was the defense. That fire led the team to the playoffs and conference championships almost every season during the mid-1970s. Quarterback Kenny "Snake" Stabler began as a scrambler, but knee injuries forced him to concentrate on passing. That became his strong suit, thanks in part to his great group of receivers. He had a Super Bowl, four Pro Bowls, two first-team All-Pro mentions, and an NFL Most Valuable Player award to his credit, among others, and he is a member of the Pro Football Hall of Fame.

Art Shell was at tackle. A phenomenal player, by the end of his playing career, he was a two-time Super Bowl champ, an eight-time Pro Bowler, and a two-time All-Pro. He, of course, went on to have a lengthy coaching career. Guard Gene Upshaw was a two-time Super Bowl champion and had six Pro Bowls and three first-team All-Pros to his credit. His younger brother, Marvin, played for several pro teams.

Fred Biletnikoff was a wide receiver and a good one, as his 589 receptions for 8,974 yards and 76 touchdowns show. Though he didn't have a lot of speed, he was agile and had great hands. A four-time Pro Bowler and first-team All Pro, he would soon be not only a Super Bowl champ but named the most valuable player of the game. Wide receiver Cliff Branch was another excellent player. One of the most effective receivers in the league, he won several awards for his work. By the end of his career, he was a three-time Super Bowl champion, a four-time Pro Bowler, and a four-time first team All-Pro.

All-Pro Dave Dalby was our center. He'd replaced Hall of Famer Jim Otto in 1972 and played with the Raiders for fourteen years without missing a game. He eventually played in three Raider Super Bowl championship teams before retiring in 1985. Unfortunately, he died in a car accident in 2002, when he was just fifty-one years old. Fullback Mark van Eeghen, who contributed greatly to our passing game, was the team's second-leading rusher during Super Bowl XI. By the time he retired, he was the Raiders' all-time leading rusher with 5,907 yards.

Halfback Clarence Davis was a decent runner and catcher. Just a couple of years earlier, his "Sea of Hands" catch finished off what is probably one of the greatest NFL games in history. Oakland was playing the Miami Dolphins, and with just two minutes remaining on the clock, Miami led, 26–19. On the Dolphins' 8-yard line, Stabler tried to hit Davis with a pass. Davis was in the end zone, but so were Dolphin defensive back Charlie Babb and linebacker Mike Kolen. All three grabbed the ball at the same time, but Davis was the one who came away with it, scoring the winning touchdown. We all thought that was kind of amazing since we usually called Davis "Hands of Wood" because he did not have good hands and often had trouble catching passes.

Running back Pete Banaszak, whom we called "Rooster," had been with the Raiders in Super Bowl II. In 1978, he also won a controversial game against the San Diego Chargers using the Holy Roller play, which is a forward fumble. In that case, the ball was picked up in the end zone by Raiders' tight end Dave Casper for a touchdown. The play is no longer legal by NFL rules.

On defense, our two lead safeties were Jack Tatum and George Atkinson. Tatum was nicknamed "the Assassin" because of his hard-hitting playing, which left a string of injuries in its wake. That began with his very first pro game—against the Baltimore Colts—during which he hit tight ends John Mackey and Tom Mitchell so hard that he knocked them out. More of that sort of behavior was to come from Tatum, and it all culminated a few years later—after I was off the team. During a game with the New England Patriots, he went to tackle Darryl Stingley and hit Stingley so hard, he was left permanently paralyzed from the chest down. The league didn't discipline Tatum for that, but it did outlaw those sorts of viciously violent tackles.

Tatum was well paired with Atkinson. While I was a freshman at Rice, Atkinson racked up a Raiders' record for punt return yardage in a game against the Buffalo Bills, and he was a great pass interceptor, but he played hard. A good example is what he did in 1975 and 1976 in games against the Pittsburgh Steelers. Both times, he smashed Lynn Swan in the back of the head with his forearm, knocking him out and giving him a concussion. I saw the second of these incidents. It happened after the play was over. Atkinson came up behind Swan, slugged him, then joined the other players who were running to the huddle.

The thing was, there were only a few officials on the field, and none of them saw the blow that felled Swan, so there were no repercussions for Atkinson. Also, this was in the days before instant replay gives officials the chance to go back and review plays and player behavior. Now, I don't want to make out that Atkinson and Tatum were the only ones doing these sorts of things. Atkinson slugging Swann became famous because it was so obvious, but a lot of guys played hard—hitting, biting, and scratching their opponents. I saw it all the time throughout the league. Every team has guys who are more fearless than others, and they're the ones you didn't mess with because they'd tear you up. Remember, this was still the days of man-to-man defense, and it was the job of a player to beat up on the guy facing him. When the ball is snapped, they're looking at the guy in front of them and thinking, *I'm going to take you out.* I suppose it was one way of eliminating a threat, and if you didn't eliminate the threat, you wouldn't be working next year.

Cornerback Skip Thomas was another fierce tackler. He had the nickname "Dr. Death," but he didn't get that from any violence on the field but because Bob "Boomer" Brown thought he looked like the cartoon character of the same name. Dave "the Ghost" Casper was at tight end, but he sometimes played on the line. He had a slow start his first year or two, but by the time I played on the team, he'd improved greatly. When he retired, he was a five-time Pro Bowler and a four-time first team All-Pro, and he was named to the NFL 1970s All-Decade Team.

Another great player was cornerback Willie Brown. His NFL career as a player ended with three Super Bowls, four Pro Bowls, and two first team All-Pro. And this isn't counting his accolades from prior years when the Raiders were playing in the AFL. Phil Villapiano was a very fast linebacker who played the strong side. He specialized in making big plays and was a four-time Pro Bowler and later a Super Bowl champ.

Ted Hendricks was another outstanding linebacker. When I was with the team, he played the weak side, but later, after Villapiano got injured, he moved to the strong side. He came from Guatemala and was the first NFL player born in that country. He'd played for the Baltimore Colts and the Green Bay Packers before joining the Raiders in 1975. Overall in his career, he chalked up four Super Bowl wins, eight Pro Bowls, four first-team All-Pro mentions, and seven AFC championships, and was named to both the NFL's 1970s and 1980s All-Decade Teams.

Willie Hall was one of our starting linebackers. He'd played college ball for the University of Southern California, where he was a college All-American. A second-round draft pick by the New Orleans Saints, he played for them for a couple of years before being acquired by the Raiders in 1975. Basically, he was used as a rusher, though he started from a linebacker position.

Defensive end Otis Sistrunk never played college ball. Instead, he went into the US Marines, so his educational background was listed in his bio as "US Mars," meaning US Marines. After he mustered out of the Marines, Sistrunk played semipro ball for a few years before he was recruited by Oakland in 1972. He was a huge guy with a bald head that became famous during a broadcast on *Monday Night Football*. The weather was cold, Sistrunk was hot, and his bald head was visibly steaming. Because of that steaming head and his listed educational background, commentator and ex–NFL player Alex Karras quipped that Sistrunk had graduated from the University of Mars. After Sistrunk retired from pro ball, he briefly became a pro wrestler.

Defensive back Neal Colzie was an excellent punt returner with 1,759 yards returned in his career. Sadly, he died relatively young from a heart attack. And last but not least were Pat Toomay, whom I'd played with on the Cowboys, and Gary Butler, my old teammate and good friend from Rice, who'd originally been drafted in the second round by Kansas City but was now with the Raiders. Gary was a great tight end and was running second or third team behind Dave Casper.

When Al Davis flew me out to Oakland, there was some question of whether I'd actually be on the team, but during my first week of working out, Gary Butler hurt his leg in practice. It wasn't a serious injury, but he wasn't going to be able to play for a week or so, which opened up a spot on the team. Fortunately for me, Al decided I was the one to fill it. I don't know what Al originally had in mind, but he put me behind Villapiano, mostly playing on special teams. He wasn't paying me much, but I was feeling pretty good, knowing I had a job playing football.

Even better, the Raiders had a good team as you can tell from the roster above. All the players were competitive and would do what it took to win, but despite that, things looked a little shaky at first. By the time I arrived, they'd only barely slipped by the Pittsburgh Steelers, 31–28, in the season opener, and soon after, they lost to New England by a single point: 35–34. After that, though, the Raiders didn't lose another game and finished the season 13–1. That wasn't solely due to me, of course, but I was making plays and putting pressure on my opponents, right alongside the team's superstars. I played my first game for them on special teams, and it was a good one for me.

The second game I played was against Philadelphia, and a couple of times when I went down on kickoffs, I didn't go as hard as I could have. Al Davis warned me to keep up the pace, and that's what made me notice that Al wasn't just the owner; he watched everything and everyone, including me. He was right, and I told him I wouldn't let it happen again. I wasn't worried because I had my stuff covered, and anyway, I was on the left side and they went down the right side. But he mentioned it to me to let me know that he wanted me to play at 100 percent, period. Now, Al liked big, strong guys, and he often looked at that over productivity. I wasn't the biggest and strongest, but on the field, I weighed 500 pounds. At least that's the way I looked at it. So Al's criticism psyched me up to go harder, and after that, I made big plays every game.

We ended up proving ourselves right up to the playoffs, in which we faced off against the New England Patriots. This was our most critical game. The first playoff game often sets the tone for the rest of the championship, and we knew that the Patriots would be a handful. Not only were their offense and defense very good, but they also had young players who played hard. We were moving the ball, but the Patriots had been making the big plays, and by the last few minutes of the fourth quarter, they were up by three points, 21–17. It looked like we were about to lose the first game of the playoffs.

With less than two minutes left, Stabler threw a pass to Biletnikoff, who was in the end zone. That play should have been automatic for the two of them, but Freddy didn't make the catch. Those of us on the sidelines were going, "Man, we can't believe it." But then, bam, the flag came out, and a penalty was called against Patriots' Ray Hamilton for roughing the passer. After that, with just fourteen seconds left, Stabler took us over the line with a one-yard touchdown run. So we barely squeaked by the Patriots, 24–21, sending us to the AFC Championship.

That was against the Pittsburgh Steelers, which was a little nerve-wracking. We were very competitive with them, always trading wins back and forth. Often it would be some miracle play that would sway the tide in one direction or another. Sometimes it might be a big play that everyone could see, and sometimes it was more subtle—something that only players and coaches might notice. As you can imagine, we were looking for something strange to happen to move the game in our direction. In our favor, we had a slightly better record that season, which put the game in Oakland, giving us home-field advantage. But the Steelers were backed by a strong reputation. Not only had they won the two previous Super Bowls, but they'd also beat the Raiders in three of the last four playoffs and had just seriously outscored both the Washington Redskins and the LosAngeles Rams during this year's playoffs.

But strong reputation or not, we intended to beat them, and this time we lucked out. Despite the Steelers' seeming dominance, a couple of their starting backs—Franco Harris and Rocky Bleier—were injured, weakening them. That gave us a definite edge, and we won, 24–7, earning us a berth in Super Bowl XI against the Minnesota Vikings, which was played on January 9, 1977 in the Rose Bowl.

Preparations

There's a two-week span between the end of the division championships and the Super Bowl, and we spent the first week at home really getting everything down and going over the other team's plays, making sure we were going to be the ones making the big plays. So we went hard to put in all our game plans and other stuff that first week.

The second week, we flew to Los Angeles, though we stayed in Newport Beach, which is forty or fifty miles southwest of LA. The place we stayed was really nice and plush, and we brought out our families. I flew my mom in, and I would have brought my girlfriend, but she was pregnant and only a month away from giving birth, so the doctors discouraged it. My dad lived in California, and he came, so I had a mini cheering squad out there for me.

We got there on a Sunday, but we didn't have curfew until Thursday, so we had time to run around and see people and have some fun. All we had to do was make practice a couple of hours in midday because we'd done all our hard work in Oakland before we went to LA and were just brushing up on everything. The organization didn't ride us but just left us alone to enjoy being in the Super Bowl. So as we got ready to play the game, we were pretty laid back, but I think the Vikings were a little uptight. Maybe that was because they'd lost the last three Super Bowls they'd played in and didn't want to lose a fourth. While we were going out during our off-hours, they stayed put. Their hotel was out in the boondocks, quite a way from LA, but it could have been in the middle of the city for all it mattered since their players weren't allowed to go anywhere except the hotel or the practice field.

Once you're going to the Super Bowl, you feel great, but we also were really confident as we approached Minnesota. We'd beaten the best teams in the NFL all through the season and the playoffs, and we felt like we could beat anybody. That didn't mean we took the Vikings lightly. Their head coach was Bud Grant, and the top of his roster was impressive. Their offense was led by quarterback Fran Tarkenton, who was, at the time, the league's all-time leader in pass completions, passing yards, and touchdown passes. At thirty-seven, he was old for pro football, but the 1976 season had been good for him, and he was a great quarterback and a formidable opponent.

They also had a great running back in Chuck Foreman, who was one of the best pass-catching backs in NFL history. He wasn't as fast as OJ and his style of playing was different, but he was like OJ in that he carried the team. His quick feet and agility earned him the nickname "the Spin Doctor." Plus, he was smart and had been playing for some time, giving him solid experience. That just makes you better because you know what to look for in your opponents. Foreman's productivity was phenomenal, and he made the list of 50 Greatest Vikings. He was asking for a million dollars a season, which we thought was crazy, but when you look at everything he did, he probably was half or more of their offense.

Another of their major offensive players was rookie wide receiver Sammy White, who made the big plays downfield. He, too, eventually made the list of the 50 Greatest Vikings. Brent McClanahan was one of their best running backs. He played his entire career—seven seasons—for the Vikings until injuries forced his retirement. He's now a high school teacher and was named the NFL Teacher of the Year in 2015, an award given to former players who have become outstanding educators.

Wide receiver Ahmad Rashad had been an All-Conference and All-American running back and was inducted into the College Football Hall of Fame. In the pros, however, he played wide receiver for several teams before he joined the Vikings. He later became a sportscaster for NBC and ABC. He also hosted the series NBA Inside Stuff for sixteen years. He's also appeared in television shows, often with his then-wife, Phylicia Rashad.

In college, offensive tackle Ron Yary had been named the Pac-8 defensive lineman of the year as a sophomore, a consensus All-American as a junior, and a unanimous All-American as a senior. That last was in 1967, and that same year, he also won the Outland Trophy and the

Knute Rockne Award. Since then, he's been inducted into the College Football Hall of Fame and the Rose Bowl Hall of Fame. He played for the Vikings for something like fourteen years, and during that time, the team chalked up eleven division titles, won the NFL championship and three NFC titles, and played in four Super Bowls. He had been an All-Pro for six seasons and second-team All-Pro, and he played in seven consecutive Pro Bowls. He has even more honors, but I'll leave it with his induction into the Pro Football Hall of Fame in 2001.

The Vikings' defense was just as great and was the league leader in fewest points allowed, earning them the nickname "Purple People Eaters." One of the most important Purple People Eater was Carl Eller, dubbed "Moose." In college, he'd played for the University of Minnesota, where he was instrumental in the team's Rose Bowl victory in 1962 and was twice named All-American. While Eller was with the Vikings, the team chalked up an impressive record of playoffs, championships, and Super Bowl appearances. He also played six Pro Bowls and is considered the Vikings' all-time sacker. He was a five-time First-team NFL, two-time Second-team All-Pro, and an AP / *Sporting News* All-NFC.

Another of the Purple People Eaters was defensive end Jim Marshall. He was one of the Vikings' oldest players, and by the time he retired, he'd played 282 consecutive games—starting in 270 of them. That's a record broken only by Brett Favre. Marshall was in two Pro Bowls and four Super Bowls, but he is perhaps best remembered for what might be the most humiliating play in NFL history. It happened in a matchup between the Vikings and the San Francisco 49ers on October 25, 1964, when Marshall recovered a fumble and ran the ball sixty-six yards for a touchdown. Believing he'd scored, he tossed away the ball, but there was a serious problem. Marshall had run in the wrong direction and was in his own team's end zone.

Right defensive tackle Alan Page also was one of the Purple People Eaters. He'd played college ball for Notre Dame, and his many awards culminated with his induction into the College Football Hall of Fame in 1993. His pro career was even more notable. He was chosen by the Vikings in the first round of the 1967 draft, and while he was with them, the team won four conference titles and one league championship, and he played in four Super Bowls. By the end of his football career, he'd earned numerous awards, was a six-time All-Pro and eleven-time All-Conference, and was voted to nine Pro Bowls.

Page's postfootball career was even more remarkable. After retiring from playing, he worked as a commentator for Turner Broadcasting System's *College Football on TBS* series and for National Public Radio, but all that was just a warm-up. During his time playing with the Vikings, he also went to the University of Minnesota Law School, from which he earned a JD. Following a similar upward trajectory as his football career, his legal career went straight to the top, first as a working attorney, then as Minnesota's assistant attorney general, and finally as an associate justice of the Minnesota Supreme Court—the first African American to fill that position.

Defensive back Nate Wright played college ball for San Diego State University, where he earned All-Conference before turning pro. He'd played for the Atlanta Falcons and the St. Louis Cardinals, and he joined the Vikings in 1971. He was never All-Pro or named to a Pro Bowl, but he was a decent pass interceptor.

Paul Krause had played wide receiver and defensive back for the University of Iowa, where he tied the Iowa record for touchdown pass receptions. He also played baseball and was drafted into the major leagues while still in college, but a shoulder injury put an end to that, and he turned to football. He started his pro football career as a second-round draft pick with the Washington Redskins, where he continued his great work at catching passes, earning him NFL Rookie of the Year and a place in the All-NFL first team. He was playing well, so it's a mystery to me why he was traded to the Vikings in 1968. I guess it was one of those cases of a coach who didn't want to promote a player even if he was doing good things for the team. Whatever the reason, the Redskins' loss was the Vikings' gain. During his time with the Vikings, Krause was known as the team's "center fielder," partly because of his background in baseball and partly for his record-breaking ability to intercept passes.

These were some of the guys we were up against.

Super Bowl XI

Super Bowl XI had a number of unique features that make handy factoids. It was the first time the Super Bowl was played in the Rose Bowl. It was the last Super Bowl played completely in daylight and the earliest to be played in the year. It also started earlier in the day than other Super Bowls. Another deviation from the norm was that singer Vicki Carr sang "America the Beautiful" instead of the national anthem—the only time that's happened. I played in the first, third, and last quarters, but while I'll go through some the game's high points, I'm not interested in giving a play-by-play commentary on it. There already are plenty of commentaries on the subject, and the game itself is on the internet. Besides, in some ways, playing a Super Bowl game is almost unimportant. It seems to go by in a flash. It's the two weeks of excitement and work that lead up to it that are most memorable—not to mention the satisfaction of winning.

We had the opening kickoff and tried to come on strong after that, but we couldn't quite score, and Errol Mann's field goal attempt from the Vikings' 12-yard line hit the goalpost. But we held them to the same standard, and the entire first quarter was head-to-head, without much headway. But that didn't mean we weren't working hard. Phil Villapiano made one of his great plays that first quarter by tackling Vikings' running back Brent McClanahan and causing him to fumble, allowing Willie Hall to recover the ball.

One play in the first quarter, though, was an embarrassment for me. The Vikings punted, and we were set up for a left return, but the ball went to the right. Neal Colzie caught it and started the return back toward the left, but near the beginning of his run, I made what might have been the biggest mistake of my career—on the field, that is.

Viking Doug Dumler, who was pretty fast, was running toward Colzie, and I knew I couldn't let him hit my boy. If you run into a guy who weighs 250, he's going to light you up. We were deep in our own territory, and Colzie might fumble, sending the ball anywhere. I cruised up next to Dumler but couldn't get in front of him. He was on my inside, and if I ran in front of him, I'd have been at a major disadvantage when I tried to block him. Colzie should have been able to see that I was setting him up, and I expected him to dip to the outside to avoid Dumler. But Colzie just kept going straight at Dumler like he was running blind. Maybe Colzie didn't see him, but the truth is, while Colzie was an experienced runner, he wasn't good at setting up players to help defend him. He was more of a straight-out kind of runner.

By now, Colzie was a little in front of me, and if he'd dipped to the left like I was setting him up to do, Dumler would have had to follow, and then, bam, I'd have put a sneak block on him. After that, Colzie could have just straightened up and headed right down the seam to the goal. Unfortunately, Colzie didn't do that, so I knew I had to hit Dumler any way I could to keep him from slamming into Colzie. I could give up a lot for the team, but I couldn't willingly give up the ball. Because Colzie didn't dip, I couldn't get a good angle on Dumler, so I had to clip him because he was a little in front of me. That let Colzie go up the seam, and he ran the ball down to about the Vikings' 30-yard line, but because I was flagged for the clip, the officials brought the ball back to our 20. The officials called "pushing in the back" on me, and it was the first bad play that I'd made.

John Madden was upset because of the penalty, but he hadn't seen what happened.

"Who did that?" he asked, and I said, "Shoot, Coach, that was me. I did it." He didn't ask for an explanation but just turned and walked away. Then everybody knew when play-by-play announcer Curt Gowdy said, "Could be Rodrigo Barnes was the guilty party on that clip. I saw number 51 down there in a hurry. He was really hustling. He does that a lot. He's a real top, special teams man, but I think that time he got there a little bit too late."

I felt awful. I knew the play hadn't gone down the way it seemed from the sidelines, so I don't think that Madden or anybody else understood why I did what I'd done. But I didn't have a choice because I wasn't going to let the guy hit Colzie head-on. Later, in second-guessing the play, I was really disappointed in myself because I shouldn't have let Dumler get in that position. Instead of being sneaky and trying to surprise him, I should have run a little faster and slid ahead of him. Second guesses are great, but they don't win games, and my penalty slowed our momentum a little. But a few plays later, I was back in form when the Vikings punted again.

"Rodrigo Barnes makes up for that clipping," Curt Gowdy announced, "by covering the punt of Ray Guy, generally considered the all-time greatest punter."

I didn't play in the second quarter, and by the time it started, neither team had scored. We quickly gained the advantage after that, though we began modestly with three points from a 24-yard field goal delivered by Mann. That was followed by several completed passes from Stabler and three carries by Carl Garrett. All that resulted in a touchdown, giving us a 10-point lead.

Another play that became infamous occurred when Vikings' wide receiver Sammy White was about to catch a pass from Fran Tarkenton. Defensive back Skip Thomas was chasing him down, but just as White was about to catch the ball, Jack Tatum, living up to his nickname, the Assassin, slammed into him, knocking off his helmet and sending it bouncing eight yards down the field. On the very next play, White lost his helmet again.

Another combination of three runs and a 17-yard pass by Stabler to Biletnikoff took us to the one-yard line, and on the next play, our running back, Pete Banaszak, took the ball into the end zone. By halftime, we'd taken the lead, 16–0.

I played a little in the third quarter, which began with more back-and-forth from both teams. Finally Mann hit a 40-yard field goal, bumping the score to 19–0. Unfortunately, we picked up another penalty when one of our linebackers, Ted Hendricks, ran into Minnesota's punter. That gave Minnesota the opportunity to make a 12-play, 68-yard drive, allowing Tarkenton to throw an 8-yard touchdown pass to Sammy White. The score now stood at 19–7 in our favor.

We managed to increase our side of the score to 26 thanks to a 48-yard reception by Biletnikoff and a quick dash across the goal line by Banaszek on the next play. A few plays later, it looked like the Vikings were going to score again, but Willie Brown intercepted a pass and ran the ball for a 75-yard touchdown, boosting the score to 32–7.

All along, I did my best to atone for my error by making four or five tackles on the special team and almost intercepting a pass in the fourth quarter. Missing that interception had two components, both funny in a sad sort of way. I was wearing a glove on my right hand, thinking it looked cute because it was black and our uniforms were black and silver. It may have looked cute, but I never should have played with it on. When I jumped up and tried to intercept the pass, the glove interfered with my grip and messed me up, so I missed the interception. The bottom line is, when things are on the line—like in a big game—don't try something new or unusual, and stick with the tried and true. If you bring in something new when you're in a crunch, it's sure to cause problems.

Curt Gowdy, like most of the fans, probably didn't realize that my glove had hampered me, but Gowdy had noticed something else.

"There's the pass nearly intercepted by number 51, Rodrigo Barnes," he said. "Old Rodrigo wants a Super Bowl score too. It was actually knocked down by one of his own men that time."

Yep, as I came down, there was own teammate, Floyd Rice, plowing right into me, trying to make sure I dropped the ball. Rice was a second-team linebacker I'd played against while I was with the Patriots and he was with the Oilers, and he was the sort to hold a grudge. We might have both been playing for the Raiders, but he didn't like me. Plus, he was so worried that I was beating him out because I had more athletic ability than he did that he frequently tried to mess with me. He was a little bigger than I was, but size doesn't matter when you have heart like I did. Some players just play good, hard football, but some of them will do petty, dirty stuff. This guy was the latter sort. On this particular play, he combined that with his dislike of me and hit me like I was on the other team, and when it was over, I just looked at him, thinking, *You're one sad joker.*

Having a teammate trying to hurt me and make me drop the ball was pretty disappointing, but I'd seen that sort of thing before. Most fans think of football as a team sport, but really it's an

"all about me" sport. It's an ego sport. It's all about the players making the big plays so they can shine in the public eye and get more money, not because the big plays help advance the team. And if you don't watch it, you can get caught up in that—often to the detriment of your own team.

Minnesota managed to squeak in another touchdown right at the end of the quarter, but the writing was on the wall since after that only twenty-five seconds remained in the game. So despite my errors, we won the Super Bowl, 32–14. Wow! Man, was I elated! I ran into the locker room and held up the number one to the camera so all those coaches and general managers who'd worked against me the past few years could see that I'd gotten to the top.

It was the Raiders' first Super Bowl win, and we partied all night and enjoyed ourselves. Al Davis was nice, and everything was wonderful. I was on top of the world and feeling great, but in the back of my mind, I had a nagging feeling that this might be my last season playing football. I was on a winning Super Bowl team, and that was great, but overall in my NFL career, I'd never really had a chance to start, to play regularly, or to put on my show and shine like I wanted.

So I was thinking that was pretty much it for me in the NFL. I'd been fortunate even to get picked up by the Raiders and the other teams after the Cowboys had tried to destroy me. They'd set me up after the strikes, and they really didn't want me back in the league. That was obvious after I was let go from the Patriots just days before they played the Cowboys and nobody stood up for me. So I was kind of finished with football—or at least the politics of it. And the league was through with me too. In the end, though, I got to the Super Bowl anyway and helped win it, so I had the last laugh. I was feeling that God had blessed me through all this mess, and I was feeling good even if this was the end of my playing days.

I flew to Houston and back into the real world. I had a future to think of. My baby's momma was about to give birth to my little girl, and I needed to decide what I was going to do. One possibility was to go back to school and meet some people while I was still a Super Bowl champ. I thought that might help me get some breaks while I got my life together. A few weeks later, on February 15, my daughter, Reca, came into my world, and that topped off everything for me.

Epilogue: The Real Game Goes On

I might have been finished as a player, but my relationship with football wasn't quite over. Between 1979 and 1981, I was an assistant coach for the Waco Hawks, a semipro team in the United States Football League. The first year I was there, we were unsuccessful, but in 1980, we won the championship.

After that, I decided to go back to school. I earned a master's degree in guidance and counseling and a second master's in administration, both from Prairie View A&M University. I took a job in education, and since then, I've worked in public education in Houston and Dallas, most recently as an assistant principal in the Garland Independent School District, which is in the Dallas area. I've also served as a motivational speaker, done program implementation and assessments, and acted as an employee-relations consultant for schools, businesses, pro athletes, and numerous organizations.

If not for the grace of God, I would never have gotten as far as I have. I probably wouldn't even have made it anywhere at all. I often wish that some things had gone differently, but that's me talking, not God. I am the property of the Most High, and he alone has my life in the palm of his hand. God tells us it's not by our efforts that we receive but by his grace. So I've prayed through my many setbacks, and I pray for the Rapture, but I rejoice in his will.

When I look at what God has granted me, I guess I can't be too disappointed. All in all, I made a difference in some ways—in college, in pro ball, and later in life. Not bad for a kid from Waco whose earliest real memories are of living in a plantation shack and housing projects. Throughout, I remain appreciative of the many opportunities I've had and the people who've helped me along the way, from folks at Rice University to all the teams who paid me to play even though I was a risk due to multiple knee injuries. Each of them was a step toward in fulfilling my goal of being on a winning Super Bowl team. There are a few thoughts I want to leave you with. They are filtered through the lens of sports, but I think they can resonate with people in most professions or walks of life.

I've spent a lot of time in this book talking about institutionalized racism and the awful tolls it takes on people who live under its weight.

What I've learned from being one of those people is that hatred and divisiveness are tools used to weaken and misdirect. Racism is really a means a prevailing class uses to maintain its money and power by distracting people from seeing what's right in front of them, leading them to choose a side that is against rather than for others. For some people, tearing down others is much easier than doing the hard work necessary to change oneself into a real winner.

When a person is young, winning is important and makes other people sit up and take notice, but you shouldn't base your notions of success and happiness on the opinions of others, especially when you're at the top of your game. That's when you really have to watch out for yourself and understand that every day is not going to be like that. There's nothing wrong with losing as long as you move on afterward. What's really important is making the correct effort because that's what transforms you into a more complete human being. You might have good games or bad, but you can't let either failure or success hinder you from moving on to the next challenge.

But life is not simply a matter of overcoming complications and problems. Doing that is often easy enough. What's more difficult is being successful, which means that you work really hard to correctly perform a particular act at a particular time. You might not have been able to perform that act before in your life, and you might not be able to do so later, but you do it at the time it needs to be done.

Being successful adds value to any game, but it requires personal discipline and effort. The more complete or better you want to be in a profession, the harder you have to work to acquire the necessary skills to function on a high level. That's not easy, no matter what profession you choose. The times I've failed was because I didn't put in the correct effort—sometimes physical, but just as often emotional or mental.

Training and skills can take you only so far, though, even when backed by determination, grit, and patience. You also have to find your talent. Talent is something God has given you: speed, quickness, deep thought, whatever. Once you've found it, it's up to you to develop it. Talent plus training, hard work, determination, grit, and patience equal exceptional skills, and these are the qualities that move you on in life, no matter what you have to face. Talent can be a double-edged sword, though, demanding that you pursue whatever it is you have.

The bottom line is that you can work at it, or you can regret it. At the end of life, you're either going to be happy that you put in the work necessary to improve yourself, or you're going to be bitter and filled with regrets.

Wherever you are, your job is to do your job. Success in any particular instance might depend on the flip of a coin, and there's no guarantee that your talent and skills will take you where you want to go. There are too many factors in life and too many people acting on their own likes and dislikes to guarantee success. You do the best you can and see what the outcome is, knowing that not everybody is going to be the star. But anybody can be the star at something if they place themselves in the right position and take up the necessary challenges. Your thing is to be ready to meet those challenges, so you do everything that is available to get in shape physically, emotionally, and mentally. This gives you the kind of confidence that leads to exceptional performance.

I tried to do exceptional things as a football player, and sometimes I succeeded. Since retiring from football, I've tried to apply the principles I learned as an athlete to shape my life. I like to think I've succeeded in living that life, at least in some measure, but no person can truly see or judge himself. For that, I leave myself in the hands and loving understanding of God.

A multiple-award-winning college football player, veteran of several NFL teams, and member of Super Bowl XI–winning Oakland Raiders, Rodrigo Barnes is in a unique position to give an insider's look at just how crazy the sport can be. But *The Bouncing Football* is more than tales of playing in the NFL. It also is a moving account of his personal development as he grew up black and poor in central Texas in the 1950s and 1960s. Through vivid stories and anecdotes that range from the inspirational to the tragic, it details his struggles to rise above the poverty and racism that immersed his community. That story continues with his acceptance to top-ranked Rice University just four years after the Civil Rights Act, where he was one of only a dozen African American students. There, he gained a deeper understanding of the personal issues shaping his life and became a crusader for civil rights on campus.

Barnes's outstanding college career sent him into the pros, where his fight for racial equality and fairness to players continued, beginning with a stint with the Dallas Cowboys under Coach Tom Landry and culminating in a berth on the Oakland Raiders for their Super Bowl XI win. Along the way are reminiscences of the coaches, the men he played with and against, and some of the plays that went down. He also gives an unstinting view of league politics, including how player strikes affected—and disaffected—the league and individual players alike. If you're a fan of pro football, this is one book you won't want to miss.

Bibliography

1. Belasco, Brown, Crabb, and Rachlin. "Vincent Leads Offense to Victory—Super Defense, Too!" *The Rice Thresher.* September 30, 1971.

2. Belasco, Marty. "Inconsistency Plagues 1971 Owls." *Sallyport,* October–November 1971.

3. Maske, Mark. "J. Taylor Stickes up for Beleaguered Dolphins." *The Washington Post.* November 2, 2006.

4. Hurford, Daphne. "I'll Do Anything I Can Get Away With." *Sports Illustrated,* July 25, 1977.

www.ingramcontent.com/pod-product-compliance
Lightning Source LLC
Chambersburg PA
CBHW051147120626
46547CB00012B/973